Effective
Group
Facilitation
in Education

Effective Group Facilitation in Education

How to Energize Meetings and Manage Difficult Groups

John Eller

CORWIN PRESS
A Sage Publications Company
Thousand Oaks, California

For information:

Corwin Press
A Sage Publications Company
2455 Teller Road
Thousand Oaks, California 91320
www.corwinpress.com

Sage Publications Ltd.
1 Oliver's Yard
55 City Road
London EC1Y 1SP
United Kingdom

Sage Publications India Pvt. Ltd.
B-42, Panchsheel Enclave
Post Box 4109
New Delhi 110 017 India

Printed in the United States of America

Library of Congress Cataloging-in-Publication Data

Eller, John, 1957-
Effective group facilitation in education: how to energize meetings and manage difficult groups / by John Eller.
    p. cm.
Includes bibliographical references (p.   ) and index.
ISBN 1-4129-0461-7 (cloth) — ISBN 1-4129-0462-5 (paper)
    1.   School management and organization. 2.   Group facilitation. 3. Educational leadership. I. Title. LB2806.E46 2004 371.2—dc22

                                                    2003025006

This book is printed on acid-free paper.

04   05   06   07   08   10   9   8   7   6   5   4   3   2   1

Acquisitions Editor:	Robert D. Clouse
Editorial Assistant:	Candice Ling
Production Editor:	Julia Parnell
Copy Editor:	Barbara Coster
Proofreader:	Kathrine Pollock
Typesetter/Designer:	C&M Digitals (P) Ltd.
Indexer:	Sylvia Coates
Cover Designer:	Tracy E. Miller
Production Artist:	Anthony Paular

Contents

Preface

So, you get to facilitate a meeting! You are working in your job assignment when your phone rings. Your supervisor describes a new team that is forming at your worksite to examine personnel operating procedures and to design a new set of procedures based on the needs of the group. He tells you that you are just the kind of person he is looking for to work with this team and help them be successful in their venture. He describes all the skills you possess and how these skills will help you in working with this team. You reply that you would be happy to work with this group.

After you finish talking to him, you begin to think about the task you have just agreed to. You know that you relate well to others, but running an entire team may be a bit overwhelming. How will you start the process? How will you keep the group on track? What will you do if you run into difficulties? As you ponder these and the other questions running through your mind, you begin to get nervous and have doubts about your ability to be successful in this assignment. You start to wish you had turned down the "opportunity."

These and many other thoughts run through the minds of people who are asked to facilitate groups in meetings and through decision-making processes. One of the most common complaints among people attending meetings is the ineffectiveness of these meetings and the manner in which the person in charge conducts them. We have all been in meetings where we have felt that our time was being wasted in nonproductive activities or in situations where team members couldn't work together to resolve an issue.

Many people are asked to lead meetings every day with little or no support or direction to help them be successful with the task. With few models of effective meeting facilitation to call on, many of these people are forced to conduct meetings with limited skills or options. This not only causes a stressful situation for the meeting leader but further reinforces the notion that meetings are a waste of time for participants. When people feel that a situation is nonproductive, their focus and commitment are diminished, causing them to get less accomplished. Now they not only think that meetings are a waste of time, but they have hard evidence in their lack of production to back up their negative thoughts.

Meetings can be conducted in a positive, productive, and efficient manner. Helping you to facilitate good meetings is the major focus of this book. While the facilitation process requires common sense, intuition, and good interpersonal skills, there are also many strategies that, if employed correctly, will enhance what you bring to the group and help make the group successful in accomplishing its designated tasks.

This book has been designed to provide assistance to those who have been charged to help groups of people work together to complete tasks, to generate new ideas, solve problems, or any of the other tasks that may have been delegated to them. It is intended to fill the gap that exists between traditional meeting facilitation and "best practice" in working with others. It also combines the knowledge I have gained in facilitating hundreds of groups and providing training and development to many facilitators over the last 25 years with research-proven psychological principles. While the book contains some theory, it has been designed as a practical guide to the facilitation process that contains enough theory to help the practitioner understand the reasons behind the strategies presented.

With the increased use of processes such as participatory management, community engagement, stakeholder involvement, and advisory councils in organizations, the productive operation of meetings is essential. While there are many sources on the market to deal with the theoretical aspects of specialized meeting components, there are few practical, comprehensive guides to cover the entire facilitation process. This book has been developed to fill that gap.

In the past, meetings were primarily conducted by those in the leadership hierarchy. Today, however, meetings can be facilitated by members from any position in the organization. I designed this book for use by meeting facilitators at any level in the organization. It should also provide assistance to meeting facilitators who are new to the process while giving ideas and extensions for those with previous facilitation experience. The book operates from the premise that the best facilitators are developed by drawing out their individual strengths and building on their base with strategies that match the needs of a particular situation. While the book contains strategies that can be quickly implemented for particular situations, it also serves as a guide for the total skill development of people who are required to facilitate multiple groups or engage in the meeting process over a long period of time.

In that spirit, anyone who works with other people can benefit from the strategies presented in this book; formal leaders, employees, parents, students, insiders, and those outside an organization can benefit from the guidance it provides. While the content is focused on strategies to make group meetings more productive, the material can also be used to improve individual working relationships as well. If a facilitator can apply a tactic to a group, using the same idea with an individual is normally not a big challenge. Since the content of the book is based on psychological principles that have been combined in ways that make them effective for group facilitation, they will also work with individuals in isolation. As you read through the material, be thinking about alternate, related applications that could benefit you outside the group facilitation process.

Even though the book was conceived for educational facilitation situations, the content can be applied to any group setting. Because of my extensive experience with educational, business, and not-for-profit organizations, the suggestions in the book can be applied to all of those settings. In order to help the reader with the transfer of the facilitation skills, the content of the book is presented in a generic fashion. Within the examples used for illustrative purposes, a variety of settings are highlighted to assist the reader in visualizing the many possibilities for use of this content. Past workshop participants have used this content to work with difficult groups of people, deescalate emotionally charged situations, confront problem employees, communicate better with family members, and develop personal coaching strategies. They were able to make these accomplishments by internalizing the facilitation material and "live it," rather than just memorize and use it for one specific situation.

This book is laid out in a manner that parallels the planning and delivery of a facilitative session, but readers should use the book in a manner that makes sense and meets the unique needs they bring to the situation.

The first part of the book deals with those aspects of the facilitation process that help a facilitator build a strong foundation for the work that is to be accomplished with a group. **Chapter 1** introduces the reader to the facilitation process and the roles and responsibilities of meeting facilitators, and highlights the differences between leading and facilitating groups. This information is foundational in nature and helps set the tone for the service that facilitators provide for teams. In **Chapter 2**, "**Get Ready, Get Set . . . ,**" a detailed background in meeting preparation is presented. Strategies and templates are provided to assist in structuring the facilitative environment for success. Crucial first steps in starting off a successful relationship with a group are discussed in **Chapter 3, "Go."** Strategies and templates are provided that will ensure that those first few minutes with a group are productive and build a positive foundation for the rest of the meeting.

The second part of the book highlights issues related to the facilitation process as it unfolds. In **Chapter 4, "Connecting All Members of the Team,"** readers find active strategies to build community and a sense of interdependence in the group that is working together. Team member interdependence refers to the condition where individuals have a balance between their individual needs and the needs of the entire group. This is a crucial area for the success of any team as it moves forward to tackle complex issues. In **Chapter 5, "Reaching Peak Performance,"** I present practical ideas to diagnose the group's energy level and then either raise or lower it, depending on the needs of the task. In some cases, groups can move too fast toward solution to think through their options carefully, while in others, the members may need a defibrillator to get their creative juices flowing. In **Chapter 6, "Working the Brain,"** ideas are presented to increase group thinking using brainstorming to deepen the group's problem-solving capacities. Finally, **Chapter 7, "Reaching the Goal,"** presents ways in which facilitators can ensure that their teams reach their intended outcomes and avoid the pitfalls that normally derail their best efforts.

The third section of this book discusses an area related to special issues in facilitation. **Chapter 8, "Putting on Your Oxygen Mask,"** describes the kinds of strategies meeting facilitators need to use in order to keep their perspective and avoid getting caught up in the emotions that normally accompany the group decision-making process. This is a crucial area for facilitators because they need to find a way to keep thinking and processing while the team is experiencing emotional ups and downs. In **Chapter 9, "Transforming a Difficult Group,"** specific ideas are presented to help turn around problematic situations and help the group get back on track toward its assigned tasks.

The role of a facilitator can be exciting as well as challenging. In the end, you provide a valuable service to the group you are facilitating as you work to make it successful in its assigned tasks. I hope you find the resources contained in this book interesting as well as helpful to you as you work with groups as a facilitator. I have tried to organize it to help take some of the stress out of the role. If you are performing your job well, your group members may think that what you do looks easy. The completion of their task and the ease with which they are able to accomplish it are two indications of a successful facilitation experience. This book represents an ongoing journey into the world of helping facilitate teams to work at their maximum capacity. I welcome your feedback, thoughts, reflections, and stories. Please feel free to contact me at jellerthree@aol.com. I can't respond to every e-mail, but know that I will continue to grow and learn from your experiences in the field with real people and situations.

Acknowledgments

The information from many sources that I have encountered over the years has been utilized to develop the strategies highlighted in this book. A few of the personal mentors who have helped me to grow and develop this content include the following:

The late Dr. Madeline Hunter and her information on teaching and learning

Dr. Ernie Stachowski and Dr. Marilyn Bates and their work on Essential Elements of Instruction and presentation skills

Dr. Arthur Costa and Dr. Robert Garmston and their extensive guidance through the Cognitive Coaching model and its related skill areas

Bruce Wellman and his extensive knowledge of coaching, its impact on the brain, and ways to use coaching in group settings

Bill Baker and his fine-tuning of the Cognitive Coaching model

Dr. George Barker and his study of Attribution Theory

Dr. Roland Barth and his focus on allowing stakeholders to solve their own problems

Michael Grinder and his use of NeuroLinguistic Programming strategies to help connect learners to instruction.

All of these authors and presenters have contributed to the growth of many individuals over the years and have given some unique piece of information or thought process to be integrated into the facilitation strategies presented in this book. In addition to these personal mentors, other authors and works have been utilized as foundational information for constructing this book or more directly in some of the activities contained in it. Material has been used or adapted from many sources, including Peter Block, Steven Covey, Max DePree, Patrick Dolan, Michael Finley, Dr. Victor Frankl, Daniel Goleman, Harvey Robins, Peter Senge, Dr. Thomas Sergiovanni, Margaret Wheatley, and others listed in the References.

I am grateful for the contributions that these people have made to my personal and professional life, and I hope that this book, the fruit of their combined influence, has an equally powerful impact on the lives of those who utilize it to improve their facilitation skills.

Corwin Press gratefully acknowledges the contributions of the following individuals:

Benjamin O. Canada
Associate Executive Director,
District Services
Texas Association of School
Boards
Austin, TX

Nancy French
Associate Research Professor
University of Colorado, Denver
Denver, CO

Cheryl Getz
Associate Dean
School of Education
University of San Diego
San Diego, CA

Steve Gruenert
Assistant Professor
Indiana State University
Terre Haute, IN

Carole Kennedy
Principal in Residence
National Board for Professional
Teaching Standards
Arlington, VA

Rob Kesselring
Director of Faculty Programs
Youth Frontiers, Inc.
Minneapolis, MN

Martha J. Larkin
Assistant Professor
State University of West Georgia
Carrollton, GA

Jill Schafer
Principal
Linwood Elementary School
Wyoming, MN

Ruth Sloot
Teacher
Lincoln Community High School
Lincoln, IL

John Washington
Assistant Superintendent
Division of Student Services &
Community Relations
Garland ISD
Garland, TX

Richard S. Yee
Assistant Principal
Morrill Middle School
San Jose, CA

About the Author

John Eller is an educator with varied experiences in working with adults over the years he has been in education. He has worked with masters students in developing professional learning communities at both Southwest Minnesota State University and St. Mary's University of Minnesota, is the Executive Director of Minnesota ASCD, was the director of the Southwest Iowa Principal's Academy, an assistant superintendent for curriculum, learning, and staff development, a principal in a variety of settings, and a secondary and elementary teacher. He works with groups to help them unleash the potential that may be locked up inside their organizations. In addition to the work he does in training and supporting facilitators, he also provides organizations assistance in the areas of dealing with difficult people; building professional learning communities; employee evaluation; conferencing skills; coaching skills; strategic planning strategies; school improvement planning and implementation; differentiated instruction; leadership for differentiation; employee recruitment, selection, and induction; supervisory skills; effective teaching strategies; and a variety of other topics pertinent to today's educators. He currently lives in the Minneapolis/St. Paul metropolitan area with his family. He has his PhD in Educational Leadership and Policy Studies from Loyola University-Chicago and his MS in Educational Leadership from the University of Nebraska-Omaha. He has authored books on substitute teaching, support materials for school bus drivers, support material for school leaders, and has assisted in the design of the e-learning communities in the areas of data-driven instruction and differentiated instruction that are currently being implemented by Sagebrush Learning and Corwin Press. He has had experience in writing e-learning course material, and coaches site leaders in their implementation efforts.

What Am I Getting Into?

What lies behind us is nothing compared to what lies within us and ahead of us.

—Anonymous

You don't invent your mission, you detect it.

—Victor Frankl

The facilitation process is rewarding and at the same time can be mentally and physically taxing. As a meeting facilitator, you serve the needs of your group members and work to help make them successful with their assigned tasks. In this introductory chapter, you learn about how facilitators serve teams, the characteristics of effective facilitators and teams, the purposes of meetings, and other foundational information about the facilitation process. In addition, you can assess your own strengths, match them to the skills required of facilitators, and plan for your professional growth in the area of facilitation. As you examine the contents of this chapter, use the following focusing questions to guide your learning:

 ◆ What is the role of a facilitator in working with a team?
 ◆ How is it different from leading a group?
 ◆ What are the advantages and disadvantages of facilitating from inside an organization?
 ◆ How is working from the inside different from working with a group as an external facilitator?

- What advantages do teams have over individuals in the decision-making process?
- What kinds of group behaviors do you directly impact as a facilitator?
- What group behaviors do you have minimal control over?
- What skills do you possess that you can transfer into your role as a facilitator?
- In what areas are you seeking to grow as a facilitator?

WHY DO WE GET PEOPLE TOGETHER TO MEET?

Organizations get people together for a variety of reasons. Historically, teams of people operated the first farms and businesses. Many of these teams consisted of extended family members, apprentices, or those who owed the owner some type of service. In today's work environment, teams are being used in a variety of operational and decision-making capacities. In their book *Why Teams Don't Work* (1995), Robbins and Finley list several of the advantages that teams have over individuals in operational and decision-making capacities. They include the following:

- Teams can improve the operating efficiency of the organization because team members are usually closer to the ultimate client than are the managers of the organization.
- Teams can improve communication because they are usually comprised of stakeholders in the enterprise.
- Teams have a broad understanding of the multiple issues that are needed to complete a task because their members are usually charged with completing these tasks.
- Teams can be creative because they are comprised of people representing a variety of perspectives on an issue.
- Teams understand all sides of the process needed to resolve an issue because their members usually represent constituents from these sides.

In thinking about facilitating teams, it is important to keep the information provided by Robbins and Finley in mind to make sure that we work to maximize the advantages that teams bring to the decision-making experience. The facilitator strategies discussed in other chapters of this book are designed to work with the natural advantages that teams bring to the process rather than in opposition to these strengths.

WHEN DO WE USE TEAMS?

The judicious leader combines the advantages of teams with the situations that most benefit from their utilization. While this decision is individual and contextual in nature, there are some generic considerations to look for when making a decision to put a team to work on an issue. Here are several for you to consider:

- ♦ When the decision or task would benefit from the broad perspective that a group could bring to the process
- ♦ If a variety of stakeholders will be directly impacted by the ultimate decision
- ♦ In situations where a stakeholder or stakeholder group threatens to sabotage a decision made, no matter what the outcome
- ♦ When the leader has a bias or predisposition toward a potential solution to a problem facing the organization
- ♦ When the leader is having trouble generating a variety of palatable solutions
- ♦ When the leader wants the impact of the solution to be shared among several stakeholder groups
- ♦ In situations where a decision will be accepted more readily by a group, since one of its members was involved in the decision
- ♦ If a decision needs to be carefully considered before settling on a solution

In all these scenarios, the broad-based power of the team is used to help make a better decision or process. Facilitators can use these considerations to their advantage when working with group members to help them work together in a productive manner. Consider the strategy employed by a facilitator (Jane) in working with a group to make a decision regarding an employee recognition program. In starting the meeting, she tells the team members why they have been asked to participate in the decision about employee recognition:

> You are here because you represent the major groups that will be directly impacted by this decision. Each of you brings a slightly different lens to this committee, but we need to find a way to combine these views in a manner that will best serve the needs of all employees.

Facilitators usually are overt and open about the processes that they are employing to work with their group. In this case, Jane let the group members understand why they were chosen and gave them permission to look at the issues from their own perspective, but she also set up the expectation that in the end, the group would be making a decision that serves the collective employees of the organization. In this example, Jane utilized a technique called framing, which is discussed in more detail in Chapter 3.

It is important to understand what kinds of decisions are best for teams to make and not to make. These kinds of decisions are situational and contextual, but the following generic ideas provide some guidance in the types of decisions to avoid having teams make:

- A decision that has already been made but needs a stamp of approval from a group
- Decisions where no real options or choices exist
- Situations where the power players want to influence a group to their way of thinking
- Difficult decisions requiring very complex problem-solving skills not yet introduced to team members
- Situations where the leaders of the organization or other entity will engage a group in a decision, and once the decision is made, change the decision, blaming the group for making the wrong decision on the issue
- Cases where no budget exists to implement the recommendations of the team
- Decisions where the group making them will be totally immune from the impact of the final outcome of the decision

All of these scenarios have a similar potential negative impact on the team making them. Asking a team to engage in a decision that is illustrated by one of the scenarios above could be perceived as condescending by that team. These kinds of tasks also waste the time of the team members. In cases such as the ones presented above, it is better to find some other mechanism or process to assist in the decision making rather than burden team members with the responsibility. Most stakeholder groups would rather hear that a decision on a topic was made without their involvement up front rather than finding out this same fact after the members have worked extensively on a committee charged with making a decision or that no real possibility existed for their decision to be implemented after they made it. Consider the following example in relation to this principle:

> I was recently asked to facilitate a group of parents in a school district who were interested in adding a new kindergarten program for the upcoming year, but the school district had no money to

implement this program. Two school board members thought that we should form a task force to brainstorm ideas for these new kindergarten options. I carefully explained the potential problems in setting these people up to think that they were going to be making a decision that could be implemented when there was no way for that to happen. These board members couldn't see the dangers of this practice. Finally, after several months of talking through the issue, the board members dropped it. We told the parents that we could not even consider the new programming ideas until our budget situation improved.

On the surface, it may seem like the actions in this example shut down out-of-the-box and innovative thinking in the school district. That was not the intent of keeping the group members from meeting. Their work was put on hold until they could make a decision that had the possibility of being implemented. This school district had been notorious for asking groups and task forces to meet to generate ideas, only to have the final recommendations shot down at the last minute because the funding needed to implement the ideas was not available. This practice had caused much discontent among stakeholders in the district and made it extremely difficult to find people willing to serve on decision-making teams.

As a facilitator, you will need to know and understand the conditions surrounding the decision you are being asked to help facilitate the group through. It will be important for your success and the success of the group that it has some potential for success. If not, you will have to work to change the parameters under which the group will be working or recommend that the decision needs to be made using some other method.

THE IMPACT OF A FACILITATOR
ON THE EFFECTIVENESS OF A GROUP

Facilitators can have a positive impact on how well a group completes its assigned tasks. Let's look at a few examples where either the presence or absence of a facilitator impacted the effectiveness of a group working on a task.

1. At a recent meeting of a school district's administrative staff, the assistant superintendent of schools asked members of the administrative team to start the meeting by sharing a current positive initiative that was being implemented at their building or in their department. There was a short period of silence and then one principal shared a success story. The assistant superintendent

listened to the story and then began to brag about how well this school was doing in its school improvement efforts. She said that the others in the room could learn from the example set by this school. She then asked for more initiatives, but no other site was willing to share an example.

2. A PTA budget committee was meeting to discuss its fundraising plan for the upcoming year. The facilitator of this committee asked the committee members to share their ideas for getting the membership of the PTA involved in the next fundraising drive. No ideas were shared immediately, so the person facilitating the meeting asked committee members to form groups of three and take 2 minutes to talk about potential ideas for this situation. At the end of the time, the facilitator asked the group members again to share ideas for the fundraising drive. This time, there were four possible strategies shared. The facilitator wrote them down on a piece of chart paper and broke the group into three large teams to talk about the merits and limitations of each strategy. At the end of the meeting, the group members had chosen one of the ideas for implementation. They had also worked out all the details regarding this idea, and it was ready to be presented to the PTA membership in the next newsletter. In past years, this committee had worked without a facilitator and had gotten into the habit of using an ineffective involvement strategy because the group was unable to generate any new, fresh ideas.

3. At an elementary school site-based management council meeting recently observed for another study, the group was engaged in a discussion involving setting the parent-teacher conference schedule. The principal of the school was leading the meeting. He asked for ideas in regard to setting the times for the conferences, and the music teacher shared a suggestion. The principal disagreed with his idea before he had finished his explanation. A classroom teacher then gave a different suggestion. The principal immediately agreed with this idea and called for a vote. Since the leader had supported this idea, a majority of the staff voted in favor of the idea. Several of the teachers on the site council were upset by this discussion and vote and were seen complaining in the parking lot outside the school about the decision and how the meeting had been run by the principal.

4. In preparing for a work team meeting, the person facilitating it was faced with a situation where one of the team members always tried to monopolize the discussion. Several of the other work team members had come to the person facilitating the meeting to share their displeasure with this person's behavior. The facilitator understood that this know-it-all at times had valuable information to share with the other members of the team but needed to find a way to channel his suggestions. She planned a strategy to begin to address the situation at the next meeting. In the meeting, she asked members to write down their ideas for their upcoming departmental goals. She then had them meet in small groups to discuss their ideas, and chose one member from each of the small groups to share their group's ideas. She purposely did not choose the know-it-all. The meeting went well as a result of her added structure. At the end of the meeting, she told the know-it-all that she understood that he had valuable information to share and was glad he allowed others to participate. Over the next few months, she worked with this person to help him find ways to positively contribute to ideas while letting others have a chance to participate as well.

In all these scenarios, the person leading the meetings was engaged in behaviors that caused certain things to occur on the team. The meetings that were conducted by facilitators had different outcomes than the meetings run by others because of the ability of the facilitators to put their personal agendas on hold in order to implement strategies designed to help make the team successful in the tasks each was attempting. In the other meetings that were conducted by nonfacilitators, problems arose. Later in this chapter we examine the specific strengths that facilitators bring to a meeting to help make it positive and productive. Let's take a look at the unique position of a facilitator and how facilitators work to make teams successful.

THE UNIQUE POSITION OF A GROUP FACILITATOR

In today's organizations, whether they be schools, service clubs, businesses, or other enterprises, many stakeholder groups are involved in helping to make decisions. In some schools, site councils assist principals in providing a broad-based perspective in light of important school decisions; in other school districts, decisions regarding specific curricular programs are being made by community-based teams. In many service clubs, their work is organized by decision-making teams. In still other settings, teams are engaged in designing and implementing effective organizational improvement processes.

These teams and others don't operate effectively on their own; they usually require the assistance of a skilled facilitator to help them work in an efficient and effective manner. Keeping this in mind, the facilitator serves a group in ways that are different from that of a typical team member. Here are some of the ways in which facilitators serve decision-making groups:

- ♦ Manage group processes
- ♦ Provide the direction or goal for the group
- ♦ Track conversations; bring the group back into focus when the conversation strays too far off topic
- ♦ Manage energy; keep it at an optimal level for effective group operation
- ♦ Provide a safe but stimulating meeting climate
- ♦ Keep the process moving along in a productive manner
- ♦ Frame and set the parameters for decisions, how group members interact, and the depth of problem analysis used in the meeting
- ♦ Act as a group coach; set the conditions for the group to see the problem, design its own solutions, and implement the plan it has designed; keep the group positive and on track
- ♦ Provide information needed by the group to complete its assignment
- ♦ Take in group energy and emotions and rechannel these to help the group stay productive
- ♦ Provide a global view of the group and its processes
- ♦ Serve the group in whatever ways are needed to help it be successful in its assignment

These service roles obviously transfer to skill sets that facilitators need in order to do a good job in working with a team. The topic of facilitator skills is explored later in this chapter.

Even though facilitation and leading are sometimes lumped together as the same process, they do have some distinct differences. Facilitators can serve a group in a way that is much different from that of a leader. Michael Doyle and David Straus, in their book *How to Make Meetings Work* (1982/1993), talk about why managers shouldn't run their own meetings and why facilitators should be enlisted to conduct fair and objective meetings. Their information has been adapted for Table 1.1 to illustrate the difference between meeting leaders and meeting facilitators. Let's examine leading and facilitating to look for similarities and differences in these two processes.

Table 1.1

Meeting Leaders	Meeting Facilitators
The leader of the meeting usually has a higher level of authority in the organization than the people being led.	The facilitator of a group may have a higher level of authority in the organization than those being led, but the positional power of this person is not used in the process.
The leader of the meeting is charged with getting the group to a certain decision or outcome.	The facilitator of the meeting has a role to serve the group being facilitated.
Meeting leaders have an interest or stake in the outcome of the decision or task the group is engaged in completing.	Meeting facilitators usually aren't interested in the specifics of the decision or task the group is engaged in completing, but rather in the integrity of the process used to reach the goal or decision.
Meeting leaders do most of the talking in a meeting.	Facilitators let the participants do most of the talking in a meeting.
The team serves the needs of the leader.	The facilitator serves the needs of the team.
The meeting leader controls most aspects of the meeting.	A meeting facilitator sets up the conditions for success, asks the group to modify these conditions if necessary.
Meeting leaders cause members to say what they think the leader wants to hear; this is the result of the hierarchy that exists on the team.	Facilitators work to draw out the true feelings of participants on pertinent issues; this is the result of the safe and open atmosphere developed by the facilitator.
Meeting leaders are more concerned about efficiency and less concerned about process.	Meeting facilitators are less concerned about efficiency and more concerned about process.

Doyle and Straus (1982/1993) talk about the dangers to teams when the manager or leader attempts to run the meetings. They say that there are just too many variables for the leader to keep track of in order to make the meeting a success. An example that they share in the book helps to make their point.

Picture yourself, for a moment, as president of the United States on the way to the airport in your limousine with your top advisers, having a last minute meeting with them. You wouldn't want to be driving the limousine at the same time, would you? Having to deal with the traffic would be a distraction, a waste of your time. In a similar way, you are too important to your group or organization to run your own meetings. Steering a meeting, like steering a car, demands total concentration. (1982, p. 34)

For most people, a day doesn't go by when they have not been involved in some sort of meeting. The types of meetings that we participate in daily can vary from a morning family discussion designed to coordinate the schedules of family members to a corporate planning session to put together the strategic plan for the upcoming fiscal year. In all these situations, communication difficulties and personal needs can get in the way of effective team operation. Facilitators serve an important role because they act as a person in the middle or a mediator to help bring out the natural effectiveness that lies within team members. Teams that have facilitators to help them through communication and decision-making processes usually find that the meeting is more efficient and the results are better than teams that are self-led. Facilitators can be members of the team or organization or come from outside a team or organization. Let's look at the topic of internal versus external facilitators.

INTERNAL VERSUS EXTERNAL FACILITATORS

The distinction between internal and external facilitators is obvious: internal facilitators come from within the organization or division, and external facilitators come from outside the group or division. Internal and external facilitators have distinct advantages and disadvantages in working with a group. You may be asked to serve a group in either or both capacities, so it is valuable to explore the advantages and disadvantages of each type of facilitator here. As you review the list in Table 1.2, pay particular attention to how you could maximize the strengths and overcome the limitations in each role.

The information presented here is designed to let you know about some of the more common problems associated with both internal and external facilitators. Use it to raise your awareness of blind spots so you can serve your groups in the most effective manner possible. Even though in some cases one type of facilitator may be better than another, in reality, both kinds of facilitators can be effective if the strengths and limitations are carefully considered. Whether you are acting as an internal or external

Table 1.2

Internal Facilitators	_External Facilitators_
Advantages	**Advantages**
Have intimate knowledge of the group and group members; can use this information to build on group strengths and work around weaknesses.	Have limited knowledge about group or group members; can come to session with no preconceived notions.
Understand the organizational culture; can use this information to establish meeting parameters.	Lack knowledge about organizational cultural limitations or weaknesses; able to approach experience without putting up roadblocks.
Are able to get a clear vision for the desired finished product through formal and informal information channels.	Have to rely on formal information channels to find out the vision for the final finished product; are able to avoid being tainted by mixed messages.
Have knowledge of past efforts in this area; can use this knowledge to avoid problems encountered in the past.	No information about past efforts or initiatives to limit the thinking of the facilitator in designing or helping a group design a solution to their assigned task.
Are able to connect with participants between sessions; can clarify issues and make modifications as needed	Can't easily connect with participants between sessions; can avoid being influenced.
Limitations	**Limitations**
Having firsthand knowledge of the group may limit the facilitator in thinking about the capacity of the group to solve problems; the facilitator may provide more assistance than is necessary to the group.	A lack of understanding of group member strengths, limitations, and previous problems may contribute to the facilitator using the wrong strategies to help them work together.
They have knowledge about the organizational culture that may cause them to work under assumptions that will limit their ability to help the group to grow.	A lack of knowledge of the organizational culture may cause the facilitator to let the group engage in previously inappropriate behaviors.
Being from inside the organization may give the facilitator too much information about conflicting visions for the final product; this may cause confusion.	Dependent on the person who contracted for the facilitation for the final product vision; this vision may be partial or inaccurate.
The group may have too much background information about the facilitator and not accept this person as their facilitator.	The group may not have a good understanding of the background and experiences of the facilitator to establish credibility.

facilitator, keep these strengths and limitations in mind as you prepare to work with your groups.

CHARACTERISTICS OF EFFECTIVE FACILITATORS

Since their backgrounds, situations, and the difficulty of their assignments vary, facilitators possess varied skill sets. However, there are several core competencies, or foundational skills, that must be in place for individuals to be able to facilitate groups effectively:

♦ The ability to put their own needs on hold to make the group successful

♦ The ability to look at the big picture in relation to the work the team is engaged in performing

♦ A solid understanding of their own strengths and limitations

♦ Strong interpersonal skills; the ability to build rapport with people quickly

♦ An understanding of the task the group is to complete; the ability to break it into parts

♦ Skill in using observation to diagnose how the team is working together; the ability to use this diagnosis to make adjustments and implement strategies to improve their working relationships

♦ The ability to temporarily suspend their opinion in order to listen to an idea or suggestion

♦ An understanding of the optimal energy level needed by a group to function well; strategies to raise or lower the group's energy level as needed

♦ The ability to observe, interpret, and act on group body language and nonverbal cues

♦ An awareness of all the energy sources, distractions, and happenings around them; the ability to act on these for the good of the group

♦ A genuine interest in helping people do their best on a task

♦ Skill in depersonalizing anger, negative comments, and other actions that may occur as the facilitator is working a group through the stages of becoming a well-functioning team

♦ The ability to know when to press the group toward task completion and when to allow it to diverge or change directions

♦ The ability to display honesty and integrity, building a sense of trust with a group

♦ The ability to adapt to group needs or changing situations

♦ An understanding of the need for emotional self-control when working with a group
♦ The ability to stay calm under pressure

Facilitators develop these and other skills through varied experiences over time. If you sincerely care about the success of the group and are able to communicate that caring to the group, you can be successful. While having a well-developed set of strategies can go a long way to making you feel competent, facilitation is a highly emotional activity. The best facilitators are in tune with their intuition and use this sense as their guide during their facilitation experiences. Your own personal intuition is something that you will have to build as you work with groups as their facilitator. Once you have this in place, the facilitator skills you want to apply to your work will naturally fall into place.

To help you take a self-inventory of your personal strengths in relation to those needed in the facilitation process, please complete this inventory. Use the results to understand what you bring to the facilitation experience and to set personal objectives for your own growth.

Taking Stock of Your Strengths

Use the template in Table 1.3 to list the personal strengths that you possess that can help you be an effective facilitator. In answering the questions, be as specific as possible. Remind yourself of these strengths when preparing to work with a group. Use your strengths to help you reach the growth objectives you have set for yourself in relation to the skills of facilitation.

YOUR MISSION AS A FACILITATOR

The role of a facilitator is one that incorporates service and task accomplishment with a greater goal—that of helping people. Many facilitators describe their work using strong emotional language because what they do can have life-changing results on their clients, both internal and external. Rather than facilitation being just a job, it is a way of life where you live the values of service and helping people to grow. In this spirit, many facilitators find it helpful to define their personal mission and design a mission statement for their work. Use the following template to help you with this task.

Table 1.3 Personal Strengths Template

How do I build rapport with others? What do I do to welcome people and help them to feel comfortable when I meet with them? What kinds of feedback have I received about my ability to connect with others?

_____
_____
_____

What strategies do I use to make changes to my plan when a shift is necessary? How do I decide when my needs should be put on hold in favor of the needs of the group? What strategies do I use to design alternative plans when a change in plans is needed? What do I do now to maintain my flexibility when working with others?

_____
_____
_____

How do I temporarily withhold my opinion in order to serve the needs of others? What strategies do I use to make sure others know that I understand their perspective on an issue? How do I balance understanding a group or an individual's perspective while getting my point across in a positive manner?

_____
_____
_____

How do I communicate my interest in helping people to be successful? How do I demonstrate my honesty and integrity in my working relationships? How do I build a sense of trust with others?

_____
_____
_____

What skills do I employ to stay calm in uncomfortable situations? How do I mediate negative situations so the negative emotions are minimized while the parties begin to work out their differences? What skills do I use to help myself get past the negative or insulting comments directed at me by others?

_____
_____
_____

How do I work through distractions toward preestablished goals? What do I use to recognize when a group is getting off task? How do I get them back on task in a positive manner?

_____
_____
_____

What kinds of strategies do I use to assess my strengths and limitations? How do I work to impact my personal and professional growth? How do I evaluate my growth efforts?

_____
_____
_____

What are my general thoughts about my skills as a facilitator?

_____
_____
_____

Table 1.4   Personal Mission Template

What are the kinds of roles and experiences that give my life meaning?

_____

_____

_____

What drew me to facilitate and serve groups?

_____

_____

_____

What lasting impacts do I want to leave with the groups I facilitate?

_____

_____

_____

How will my interests, strengths, and passions make these impacts come true?

_____

_____

_____

Personal Mission Template

Take some time to reflect on your motivation for facilitation and the impact you want your efforts to have on the groups that you serve. After you complete the responses to the prompts, design a facilitator mission statement (Table 1.4) that you can share with the groups you work with in the future.

Design a personal mission statement that incorporates your reflections from above and reflects the following:

♦ Clarifies what is important to you in working with others
♦ Provides a mental picture of what you are about
♦ Communicates the emotional component of your focus on facilitation

Personal and Professional Growth-Planning Template

Use the planning template in Table 1.5 to help you as you set personal and professional goals for your role as a facilitator. Complete your plan using the grid in Table 1.6.

Table 1.5   Personal and Professional Growth-Planning Template

List your strengths and the gifts you bring to the facilitation process.

_____

_____

_____

What are the strengths that you see as essential to be an effective facilitator?

_____

_____

_____

What is the gap between your present skills and the skills you see as essential to effective facilitation?

_____

_____

_____

Write down your general goals for your growth as a facilitator.

_____

_____

_____

Table 1.6

Goal Activity	Specific Skill	Method to Attain Skill	Timeline	Data to Verify Skill Attainment

SUMMARY

In this beginning chapter, we have examined the background of facilitation, the roles and strengths of facilitators, and I have provided opportunities for you to think about how you fit into the role of a facilitator. The core of facilitation revolves around the ability of those interested in serving groups in this manner to connect emotionally with the groups and help their members channel their strengths and talents to accomplish their assigned tasks. This chapter is titled "What Am I Getting Into?" because it is crucial that those engaging in the practice of facilitation know and understand its components, its advantages, and its requirements. Once these elements are clear, a person can clearly serve the needs of the groups that need the services a facilitator can offer. In Chapter 2, "Get Ready, Get Set . . . ," we examine strategies that make or break facilitators and the planning they engage in when getting ready to work with a group. Enjoy your journey as a facilitator—it is demanding as well as rewarding.

Get Ready, Get Set . . .

If we live out of our memory, we're tied to the past and to that which is finite. When we live out of our imagination, we're tied to that which is infinite.

—Steven R. Covey

Success is to be measured not so much by the position that one has reached in life as by the obstacles that one has overcome while trying to succeed.

—Booker T. Washington

Planning is an essential skill for successful meeting facilitators. Unlike a presentation or other more structured meeting, a facilitated meeting can have a certain element of unpredictability. Facilitated meetings are designed to draw from participants rather than give to them. They are similar in nature to constructivists teaching lessons, where teachers have an overall learning objective in mind but construct the learning using the strengths of the students and the prior knowledge they bring to the classroom. A facilitator may conduct a meeting that seems loosely organized, but very detailed planning normally acts as a foundation to the meeting and helps keep a group on track. A facilitator needs to have a complete and detailed plan that includes alternatives if the original agenda needs to be adjusted. Even though the facilitator's plan is very detailed, it will look loose and unstructured to participants. This almost effortless look is the result of careful and purposeful planning.

This chapter explores some of the basics a facilitator needs to consider in planning a session with a group or team. As you read the material in the chapter, use the following focusing questions to guide your learning:

♦ What are the major areas that need attention in the planning process?
♦ What is the purpose of the agenda? How can an agenda be constructed that keeps the group members focused while allowing them flexibility to complete their tasks?
♦ What can the facilitator do to break down the tasks and processes into small, attainable parts for the team?
♦ How can a facilitator work with a group to construct the meeting agenda?
♦ What can a facilitator do to make directions easier to follow by participants?

THE IMPORTANCE OF PLANNING TO A SUCCESSFUL SESSION

Obviously, planning is important in getting ready for a facilitative experience. Facilitators are the "drivers of the meeting limousine," as was discussed in an example in Chapter 1. As the drivers, they are responsible for the group and themselves during the meeting. This means that they need to plan to take care of getting all parties to the meeting goals or outcomes, getting them there safely, getting them there efficiently, and helping them to learn something along the way. Facilitators, just like limousine drivers, have an extensive knowledge base to draw from when planning "the trip." What components comprise this knowledge base? How should the facilitator's knowledge base impact the planning needed for a successful meeting? Robert Garmston and Bruce Wellman, in their book *The Adaptive School: A Sourcebook for Developing Collaborative Groups* (1997), share the information contained in Table 2.1 in relation to the four major areas of a facilitator's knowledge base.

Let's take a closer look at these knowledge base areas and see how they impact the planning of meetings by facilitators.

Facilitator Knowledge Bases

Maps

Maps provide the basic structure to the meeting. They include the overall meeting goals, accomplishment of certain tasks, and team

Table 2.1   Facilitator Knowledge Bases

Maps	Self
Facilitators seek to understand meetings and make decisions affecting meeting dynamics with the aid of four types of mental modes: Universal meeting goals Structures for meeting success Energy management Principles of effective meeting transactions, information processing, and interventions	Facilitators' most sensitive and critical asset is themselves. Self-knowledge of cognitive style, educational beliefs, emotional states, intentions, strengths, and limitations permits facilitation decisions to be based on group needs rather than personal preferences
Strategies and moves	**Groups**
Facilitators manage and direct meeting processes. They know and use a range of facilitation strategies and moves to manage group energy, information, and action.	Although all groups have common tendencies, each group has unique characteristics that facilitators must take into account: culture, developmental level, group dynamics and history, relationship with facilitator, external environment, and conflicting demands

relationship outcomes. In this area, facilitators need to make sure that the group accomplishes the task it has been assigned in an efficient and timely manner. Transitions from one part of the meeting to the next are considered, strategies to keep the group processing and thinking during the meeting are thought through, and ways to step in when the meeting takes an unexpected downturn are planned. The facilitator uses this preliminary map as a guide to keep the meeting on track and focused. The following example illustrates how this works in practice:

David, a facilitator working with a site-based decision-making team, has thought through his plan for a session he is conducting on Tuesday at a school. He has used the notes he gathered from the last meeting to establish a set of preliminary goals for this meeting. His goals include some for the task the group needs to accomplish and some related to how members communicate with each other. In addition to these goals, he lays out the room arrangement and designs his opening activity. He wants to be able to use the opener to change the team members' thought pattern about the problem they are working to solve today, so he will show them a short video clip to help them see how another team thought through its solution to a complex problem. He has also thought about how he wants to get the group back in a timely manner from its 10-minute break. In the past, the group has had a problem returning back on time from breaks.

After he meets with a small group of representatives from the team he will be facilitating to get their feedback on his plan, he draws a sketch of the plan so he has something he can refer to during the session to make sure he stays on track as he works with this group.

In this example, David literally draws himself a map to help him visualize where he is going with the group in the meeting. Facilitators use a variety of strategies to help them stay on track; several of these are shared later in this chapter. The main point to remember here is that the map of the session is important because it keeps you and the group on track for success.

Strategies and Moves

In this knowledge area, the facilitator needs to think about what activities and strategies are well understood and hold promise for helping this group to be productive. This book is filled with strategies that are designed to help a group in thinking and processing together as a team. Garmston and Wellman (1999) refer to moves as quick remarks or behaviors that are made to intervene, amplify, direct, or teach a group about self-management. Strategies and moves are illustrated in the following example:

As she was working with a group, Paula had the members involved in brainstorming (a strategy) possible solutions to a problem she was facing. One of the ground rules she shared was that in brainstorming, no evaluative statement could be made about any of the suggestions until all of the possible ideas were listed on the chart. Once this had been accomplished, she would have the group evaluate the ideas using an inquiry process (a strategy). After two ideas were listed on the chart, several members of the team started to share why these ideas wouldn't work in the situation this team was facing. Paula gestured for the group to stop, and then said, "Remember, we can't comment until all ideas are up on the chart. If we do, it will interfere with our ability to get lots of ideas to consider in selecting our solution to the problem we face" (a move).

In her planning, Paula had thought about how she would handle the situation if the group didn't follow the rules of brainstorming during the meeting. She was able to quickly initiate a move that got the group back on task immediately with little disruption. She instituted her move directly and in a confident manner. The group clearly understood that she was in charge of the brainstorming activity and came back into line with her expectations.

Self

Facilitators need to examine their skills and strengths in relation to planning for an upcoming meeting. They should ask questions such as the following:

- How grounded am I in suspending my personal judgment in order to help the group to solve its own problems?
- How will I react if members begin to argue and get out of control?
- How will I feel if a team member verbally attacks me while I am facilitating?
- How well can I stay on track during the meeting?
- How will I call to mind strategies to help the group work through conflict if it occurs in the middle of the session?

These and other considerations need to be carefully thought through in planning a facilitative meeting by the person doing the facilitating. Some facilitators use a template such as the Personal Strengths Template (Table 1.3) from Chapter 1 to help them identify their personal and professional strengths; others use a variety of alternative methods to identify their strengths and limitations. Whatever the method used to get in touch with you as a person, it is important to consider what you bring to the table when planning a meeting. In the following example, look for evidence of personal awareness in the planning of the meeting:

Ben was working with a school board in its annual strategic planning session. He knew that he would have a hard time keeping the group on time as it met to discuss its issues for the upcoming year. To help him stay on track, Ben planned two strategies: he printed the exact times the board needed to spend on each topic of the agenda right on the agenda, and he set a timer that would go off when the group had 1 minute left of the time that it had designated for each agenda item. These two strategies, along with enlisting the assistance of the group at the start of the meeting, kept Ben on track and on time during the entire meeting.

Groups

Using group knowledge helps ensure that the meeting will be conducted in a way that best serves its needs. Facilitators should ask themselves questions such as the following:

♦ What seems to anger this group?
♦ What seems to energize this group?
♦ When is the group most productive?
♦ When is the group least productive?
♦ How do the members of this team best work together?
♦ How long can the team work before the members need a break?
♦ Which members of this team are not yet able to work together in a positive manner?

Generating a list of group characteristics can be helpful in setting up the conditions for success in relation to team member needs. Look at the following example and see how the facilitator used team member information to set up the conditions for success at a recent meeting:

In preparing for a meeting of district bus drivers, Tom thought about how group members normally reacted when they were asked to sit still for an extended period of time. Taking this into consideration, he took the meeting time and broke it into parts so that the drivers were required to sit and listen for only 10 minutes at a time. After he presented some introductory information to the group, he had the members meet in randomly assigned teams for 10 minutes to discuss the information. This meeting was conducted standing, so that the team members understood that it would be short in duration. After the next information session, he had the drivers walk around the room with a partner to discuss the major points they had heard about in the meeting so far. Tom found that by varying the activity level of the group, he was able to keep almost everyone focused and on track during the entire session.

Planning Checklists

Many facilitators find that a simple checklist helps them to track all the considerations they need to keep in mind when planning a meeting with a group. Some facilitators develop their own, while others use a standard format and adapt it when special conditions arise. Two checklists (Tables 2.2 and 2.3) are provided here. Table 2.2 is based on the work of Garmston and Wellman (1999), and Table 2.3 is based on the work of Justice and Jamieson (1999). These tables can be used as they are shown here or adapted as needed to meet the unique needs of a team situation.

FACTORS TO TAKE INTO CONSIDERATION WHEN PLANNING MEETINGS

The planning templates and checklist in Tables 2.1, 2.2, and 2.3 list a variety of ideas and components that need to be considered in thinking about getting ready for a meeting. Many facilitators have a list of considerations that they use when preparing for meetings. Here is a sample of some areas of facilitator consideration for meeting planning:

♦ Group psychological needs (a clear direction for the meeting, a safe environment for dialogue to occur, a welcoming atmosphere, physical comfort and other needs of the group)
♦ A strategy to welcome and connect participants at the beginning of the meeting
♦ The time of day for the meeting
♦ Working with people who are late to the meeting
♦ The purpose of the meeting (decision making, advisory, fact finding, etc.)
♦ The relationships/dynamics between the group members
♦ The arrangement of the physical space
♦ The information needs of the team
♦ Matching your strengths to group needs and strategies
♦ Time management
♦ Dealing with distractions or diversions

Group Psychological Needs

Groups of people come to meetings with certain needs that if addressed will help them work together in a productive manner. These needs include things such as a clear direction for the meeting, a safe environment, parameters for their involvement on the team, a clear end point, and the feeling that their ideas have value. These needs should be identified in the planning process so that the facilitator can put strategies in place to address them. There are as many ways to

Table 2.2   Checklist 1 for Meeting Planning

Facilitator _____	Session objectives _____
Meeting date _____	_____

Maps

The meeting objectives are identified and written down.
Meeting structures have been identified to start the meeting on a positive note such as opening activities, the optimal room arrangement, and posting ground rules for the meeting. These structures ensure a positive start to the meeting.
List examples: _____
_____
_____
_____

Draw a map of the room arrangement, taking into account the needs of participants to see the facilitator, hold break-out sessions, and be in close physical proximity to each other.

Strategies and Moves

Strategies and activities to facilitate group processing have been identified and written down in advance. List examples and conditions for their use:
_____
_____
_____
_____

Self

Strengths and limitations have been identified. List examples of strategies to maximize strengths and minimize limitations:
_____
_____
_____

Groups

Key group behaviors such as development level, ability to stay on task, group history, group dynamics, and conflicting demands have been identified, and strategies are in place to maximize the group's success. Examples are listed:
_____
_____
_____

Note: Based on Garmston & Wellman (1999).

Table 2.3   Checklist 2 for Meeting Planning

Purposes and Outcomes

What is (are) the purpose(s) of the meeting? List them here_____

_____

What are the intended outcomes of the meeting? What evidence will you gather so that you know that you have reached these outcomes? List examples here:_____

_____

_____

Who makes the decision regarding the outcomes and purposes of the meeting?

Meeting Participation

Is the group a primary decision-making body or is it acting in an advisory capacity?

Who is primarily responsible for ensuring that the outcomes of the meeting are attained? Who is the meeting leader?

Who has a significant interest in the outcomes of the meeting? Who might block the implementations of the recommendations of the group?

To whom must decisions of the group be communicated, and when do they need to be communicated?

Who should be invited to attend the meeting?

Who on the team has expert knowledge about the topics to be discussed?

Length and Location

How many hours might be required for the team to accomplish its assigned task?

How much time should be allotted to the various sections of the meeting?

Where will the meeting be held in order to maximize the energy of the team?

Meeting Prework

Are there any materials that should be distributed to participants in advance of the meeting that would make their work easier or save time? List them here:_____

_____

_____

(Continued)

Table 2.3   (Continued)

Facilitation Roles

Which of the following roles will be used in this meeting, and who will serve in each of the positions?

Group recorder: Poster or chart paper
Meeting recorder: Official minutes
Timekeeper
Small group facilitators. List them here: _____

_____

Equipment operator
Others. List them here: _____

_____

Decision Modes

What specific decision-making modes will be used by this group?
Absolute consensus (all must agree to support a decision)
Modified consensus (all must be willing to support or live with decisions
Consultative (leader decides following consultation with group)
Consultative consensus (leader consults with group, seeks consensus, and makes decision)
Voting (secret ballot, show of hands, etc., and majority, two thirds, etc.)

Reviews and Approvals

To whom must these recommendations be delivered for review and approval?

What is the deadline for the plans to be submitted for review and approval?

Equipment Required

What kinds of equipment will be required for this meeting?

Chart tablet and markers
Overhead projector
Storyboards
Dry-erase board and markers

Table 2.3

Laptop computer and projector
Microphone
Manipulative objects to assist participants in their thinking
Objects for participants to construct models of their thinking
Proper sized chairs and tables
Sticky note pads
Markers for participant drawings and constructions
Boom box or CD player for tone-setting music
Tripods for displays of norms, past work, etc.

Participant Count/Room Arrangement

How many people are expected to attend?
What room arrangement will work best for participant thinking and processing? Include a drawing of the proposed room arrangement.

Room and Facility Checkout Prior to Meeting

Is there room to post charts and posters? Are there restrictions on hanging paper posters with tape?
Is there adequate room to facilitate participant comfort?
Can observers be kept separate from meeting participants?
Are there spaces for breakout and small group work?
Where will food and refreshments be served?
Is there a phone in the room? How can it be turned off to avoid distractions during the meeting?
How is the temperature and airflow regulated so that everyone will be comfortable during the session?
When do you want messages to be delivered to meeting participants?
Are there potential structures or situations that could be distracting during the meeting? (Do bells sound at regular intervals? Is there a room adjacent to the one you are meeting in with unusually loud noise or a high traffic level?)
Is the equipment you need in working order? Is it in the right location to help you be effective?
How much in advance of the meeting is the room available for you to enter and get set up?

Note: Based on Justice & Jamieson (1999).

identify needs as there are facilitators, but among the most commonly used include

♦ Conducting interviews with group members before a meeting to ask them what specific needs may be present in the group
♦ Administering a survey to team members before the session
♦ Talking to other people who have worked with these people in the past
♦ The facilitator identifying a core set of needs/issues commonly faced when working with a group of similar makeup

Whatever the method used, it's important to spend some time thinking through the psychological needs of the group as a part of the planning process. Here are some to consider.

A Strategy to Connect Members to the Meeting or the Content to Be Discussed in the Meeting

The importance of setting a positive, productive tone at the beginning of a meeting cannot be diminished. If you lose the group members during the first few minutes, it is almost impossible to get them back later. Here are a few ideas to start a meeting and connect people to that meeting or the content to be discussed at the meeting:

♦ Posting "welcome" signs
♦ Greeting team members at the door
♦ Playing energizing music as people come in the room (more details in Chapter 3)
♦ Involving the group in an icebreaker activity
♦ Designating members of the team to welcome others as they arrive
♦ Starting the meeting with a novelty such as a video clip or interesting cartoon (more on an advanced use of cartoons in Chapter 3)
♦ Involving the group in a movement activity or song right from the start of the meeting

The Complexity of the Decision or Dialogue of the Meeting

If the group members are involved in a simple decision, they will need less support or structure than if they are working on a more complex decision. This element goes hand in hand with the reason why the group is meeting; meeting to make a decision is more complex than meeting to gather facts about a situation.

The Arrangement of the Physical Space to Maximize Involvement

While the physical arrangement of the room is based, in part, on the preferences of the group and the facilitator, there are some arrangements that promote certain types of group interactions better than others. Keep these ideas in mind when designing the physical space of the meeting room:

♦ Provide ample room to address the participants' comfort while preserving the coziness of the space. If the space is too large, the group members can become disconnected from each other.

♦ Designate a separate area for the meeting participants and for the "observers" of the process.

♦ Make sure that all the team members can see the facilitator.

♦ Use just enough chairs to seat the participants. Too many chairs make members feel disconnected from others on the team.

♦ Provide for "break out" or "thinking" areas within the room to allow team members to solve short-term problems without having to leave the room. This helps to save time and builds a connected group.

♦ Plan for the use of chart paper to capture the work of the group; plan ahead to make sure there is ample room for posting, and be sure to post the ideas captured on the chart paper in a logical, linear sequence to help your participants track the information from the meeting.

♦ Avoid positioning participants so they can look out any windows that exist in the meeting room.

♦ Set up the room so that it can be quickly rearranged for small group activity, work groups, and so on.

♦ If a meal will be served as a part of the meeting, try to have separate tables in place for eating; this helps people focus on their work and separate it from eating.

♦ Provide an open area to allow for participation and movement activities.

♦ If the room where the meeting is being held has hosted other negative meetings, it may be necessary to decontaminate it. This can be done by arranging it in a different manner than it was arranged during the negative meeting, placing posters or colored paper on the walls, or by verbally acknowledging the contamination and helping team members to think about removing it from the room.

Figures 2.1, 2.2, 2.3, 2.4, and 2.5 show some common room arrangements that facilitators use to conduct meetings.

Figure 2.1

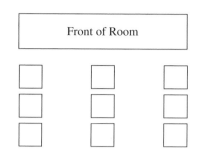

Classroom Setting: Promotes individualism, listening, sidebar conversations
Minimizes group interaction, cooperation

Figure 2.2

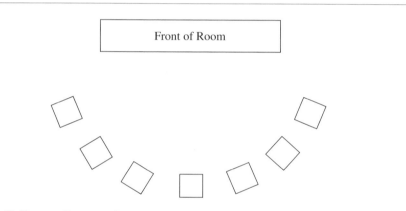

Half moon: Promotes focus on center, group involvement, some interaction
Minimizes side bar conversations, passive involvement

Figure 2.3

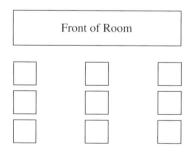

Classroom Setting: Promotes individualism, listening, sidebar conversations
Minimizes group interaction, cooperation

Figure 2.4

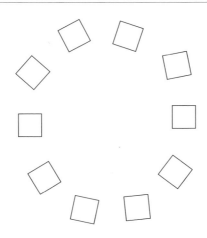

Circular or oval: Promotes group focus, equality of members, group discussion
Minimizes individual focus, the ability to disengage from the process

Figure 2.5

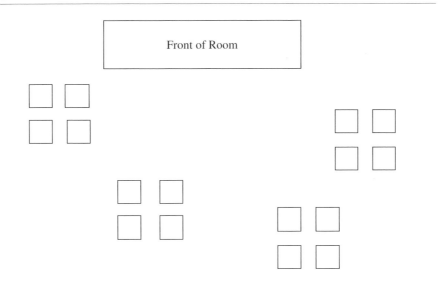

Cluster groups: Promotes small team connections, participation, multiple agendas
Minimizes a central focus, lack of participation

IMPORTANCE OF AN
AGENDA TO A SUCCESSFUL MEETING

An agenda serves an important purpose for a meeting. It provides a guide
for the group members to follow as they work together. An agenda also lets
people format their thinking for the upcoming task. When people look at
an agenda and it shows four items that are going to be discussed over the

next 2 hours, they are able to think about dividing their attention between the four items. Without an agenda, people may have a hard time determining the focus of the meeting.

An agenda also lets people decide where they will specifically focus their energy during the session. For example, Items 1 and 3 on an agenda may be more interesting to a person than Items 2 and 4. This person decides to actively participate in the agenda items that are most interesting and to have a little less focus on the other agenda items. An agenda is a crucial component to an effective meeting and one planning component that should never be overlooked by a facilitator.

Facilitator-Developed Agendas

The agenda for a meeting is normally developed by the group facilitator. The agenda is developed using what was learned about the group at the last meeting or from discussions with either a representative group of the team or the person ultimately responsible for the work this team is required to accomplish. In either case, there are some basic steps the facilitator needs to follow in order to develop a good agenda for the meeting. They are as follows:

- Identify the outcomes or goals for the meeting. Be sure to identify both task completion outcomes and group/team relationship goals. As the meeting unfolds, you will be helping the group to complete these goals and gathering data to let you know when the group has reached them.
- Break the goals down into parts so that you can introduce them and help the group accomplish these goals part by part. A guide for breaking goals into parts is included later in this chapter.
- Identify the processes that are required for each item that is being considered for placement on the agenda. If team members are engaged in evaluating problem solutions from a brainstormed list, the process they will engage in is dialogue. If they are learning new information, they will be engaged in listening. Each of these processes takes a different amount of concentration and time on the agenda.
- Once the preliminary agenda items have been listed, the amount of time required to complete each should be identified. The total for all the agenda items should be calculated. If the total time needed does not equal the time allocated for the meeting, either the meeting needs to be lengthened or the agenda trimmed. In trimming the list, prioritize the items and delete those items that can be accomplished in another manner. Be honest about the time needed

to complete the remaining agenda items. Don't think that the group can move faster through an agenda or an item than the required processing dictates. A realistic and accurate assessment of the time required to complete agenda items helps to avoid cramming items together and having to rush through important agenda components.

♦ Share the rough agenda with team representatives or the person responsible for the team for feedback. Make the necessary adjustments and distribute the agenda as needed.

Group-Developed Agendas

In recent times, many facilitators have involved their groups in developing the agenda for a meeting. This practice makes sense, since a group that develops the meeting agenda has more ownership for it than when one is imposed from an outside source. Facilitating the development of an agenda, however, is not an easy task. It takes some level of sophistication to move a group toward the agenda it needs to be productive. Be sure to check with the person who is responsible for the group to determine if there are any parameters or restrictions in the topics that need to be considered in developing the final agenda.

If assisting the team in developing the meeting agenda is an option, keep the following points in mind:

♦ Think about all the tasks or outcomes that the group members will be attempting to accomplish during their time together. These outcomes can include both the tasks they have been asked to complete and the group relationship skills that they need to improve. Be honest with the group about what needs to be accomplished in these areas and what can be accomplished in the time they have to meet.

♦ Analyze the decision-making capacity of the team developing the agenda. If the group has the skills to do even a portion of the task, it is worth the time and effort. If the group will break down and get into an argument as a result of working on the agenda, it might not be worth the effort.

♦ Decide if the team will grow as a result of the agenda development process. If there's something to be gained as a result of setting the agenda, it may be a worthwhile task; if the process will create problems, it will not be worth the effort.

When thinking about helping a team to set its own agenda, many facilitators have found the following template helpful:

1. Clearly identify the outcomes and objectives for the meeting and for the team participating in the meeting.

2. Think through any required agenda items and communicate those up front to the team.

3. Ask team members to brainstorm a list of agenda items that relate to the objectives and outcomes identified in Step 1 of this process that they would like to explore during their time together; as members brainstorm, they should not comment or evaluate any of the suggestions. Their job is just to generate a list of possible ideas.

4. Once a complete list is generated, have team members evaluate possible choices and develop a priority rating for these items. It is at this point that team members remove low priority items.

5. Ask team members to estimate the time needed to fully explore each item on the agenda. Assign those times to the items identified. Ask the group to evaluate its list to see if there will be enough time to deal with the identified items. If not, ask the team members to reprioritize the agenda and eliminate items that have a low priority.

Agenda Development Template

Table 2.4 is an example of a planning template used by one facilitator to design a meeting. Table 2.5 is a blank copy for your use.

Facilitators can use a variety of agenda formats with groups to facilitate meetings. Two general types are highlighted: agendas with tight timelines and those with general, loose timelines.

Specific Agenda With Tight Timelines

Groups can benefit from an agenda that lists specific times for each item on the agenda. This type of agenda can keep a group moving forward by not allowing it to get stuck on any one item for an extended period of time. It also allows the facilitator to schedule time for specific items where more time is needed by the group. For example, for a group that has had difficulty in its working relationships in the past, the facilitator may reduce the total number of agenda items but build in more time for the warm-up section. The facilitator may examine the draft agenda and reduce the time allocated for an item that may have caused this team difficulty in the past. Here is an example of an agenda that reflects these time priorities:

Table 2.4

Activity	Process	Time Needed	Resources	Who is Responsible for Activity
1. Opening	Discussion and sharing Foundation-setting activity Ask participants to share: • Name/role • A time when they found benefit in setting priorities • A hope for this meeting	15 minutes	Chart paper and markers for writing down the directions	Facilitator
2. Clarification of task and overview of timeline	Presentation and questions PowerPoint presentation, allow the group to ask questions	20 minutes	Handouts of presentation, computer, projector, chart paper and markers to write down questions	Assistant superintendent
3. Presentation of present budget, presentation of new fiscal budget, linking resources with needs	Presentation discussion, questions Present written materials, organize people into teams to discuss information, designate note keeper to write down major discussion points, and present finding to entire group	30 minutes	Budget handouts, chart paper and markers	Facilitator for entire process, small group leaders for discussions

Table 2.5

Meeting Agenda   **Date/time** _____

Meeting Outcomes _____

_____

Activity	Process	Time Needed	Resources	Who is Responsible for Activity
1.				
2.				
3.				
4.				
5.				

- ◆ 8:00-8:30   Opening activity (this activity had more time allocated to it since it contained processes that the team needed to learn how to work together effectively)
- ◆ 8:30-8:45   Information about the high school scheduling process
- ◆ 8:45-9:45   Presentations by high school departments to provide team members with information about student registration patterns and needs
- ◆ 9:45-10:00   Break
- ◆ 10:00-10:15   Questions/clarifications (this is an area where the team members have attacked each other in the past. The facilitator reduced the time given for this task and developed a procedure to productively work these members through the process)
- ◆ 10:15-12:00   Preliminary recommendations in regard to high school schedule

In setting up this agenda, Barbara reduced the time for the item on clarification of suggestions in order to help the team work through it in a productive manner. The strategy Barbara designed to deal with questions/clarifications asked team members to write out their concerns, then meet in small groups to discuss them. Once they had been discussed in the small groups, she brought everyone back together for a large group discussion of the same issues. By reducing the time for this part of the discussion, she hoped that she could keep the group positive for a short time. As she continued to work with this group, she gradually increased the time they spent discussing and clarifying the group's ideas. Barbara built on their previous successes as she continued to work with them.

In another situation, Howard found that his team spent too much time in meetings on trivial issues such as complaining about the working conditions of the school. Here is the agenda he developed for this team:

- ◆ 8:00-8:10   Venting
- ◆ 8:10-8:20   Overview of the meeting agenda
- ◆ 8:20-10:00   Information gathering
- ◆ 10:00-10:15   Break
- ◆ 10:15-12:00   Decision-making/communication strategies

Howard decided to hold the venting session before the formal start of the meeting, since in the past team members had been known for coming to the meeting a few minutes late. At first, he noticed that team members came right at the start of the meeting in order to vent their thoughts. He also noticed that during the first session, some participants wanted to vent beyond the allotted time. Howard had to hold firm to the 10-minute time schedule. Over time, he noticed less venting, and eventually he was able to replace the 10-minute venting section of the agenda with a section where participants were able to share positive stories and good news. The specific nature of the agenda helped to structure the behaviors of the meeting participants in a positive manner.

General, Less Specific Agenda

At times, participants can benefit when the facilitator develops and follows a general agenda. This type of agenda provides members with a general direction to the meeting but does not specify exact times for each item. This type of agenda allows for flexibility on the part of the facilitator and the group in the time that is allotted for each item. If a group is engaged deeply in discussion of an issue, the facilitator has the option to extend the time spent on this activity. A general agenda can help group members who are very concerned with specifics and get nervous when they begin to go over the assigned times on a normal agenda. Here's an example of a general agenda:

- Opening activity
- Information about the high school scheduling process
- Presentations by high school departments to provide team members with information about student registration patterns and needs
- Break
- Questions/clarifications
- Preliminary recommendations in regard to high school schedule

Even though this agenda has the same items on it that were presented earlier, it is different because it is more general in nature. This flexibility allows the team to spend more or less time on specific agenda items as need be. The facilitator will need to keep the group moving along, adjust the time spent on the remaining agenda items, or remove some items from the agenda in order to finish within the time allotted for the meeting.

BREAKING THE MEETING TASKS INTO PARTS

In effectively planning a meeting, it is important for the facilitator to be able to break the goals and outcomes of the meeting into small enough parts for the group to be able to successfully complete them during the meeting. This is similar to the process people use when they cut up their food before eating it. If the food were not cut into small parts, they could choke on the large pieces they were trying to swallow. The tasks, goals, and outcomes for a meeting also need to be broken into small parts so that the members don't get bogged down at the meeting.

In breaking up the meeting content, there are steps that the facilitator must go through to make sure the pieces of content to be discussed at the meeting are the right size for the group in order for them to be successful. Here are the steps for breaking down the content of the meeting:

1. **List all the objectives or outcomes for the upcoming meeting.**

2. **Separate the outcomes into categories based on their respective impact on the meeting.** For example, list all the outcomes related to the tasks the group has been charged with completing on one category, all the outcomes that relate to interpersonal skills the group needs to learn in another category, and so on.

3. **Pick one of the outcomes you have written in its own category; list all the component or subbehaviors that would be required to be completed in order to be successful with that outcome.**

4. **Using the list of outcome components or subbehaviors generated in Step 3, order them based on your understanding of which ones need to be accomplished before moving on to the more complex behaviors.** For example, a group may need to understand all components of a problem before moving into the generation of solutions for that problem. Once this order has been established, the facilitator can begin to address the subcomponents in a logical sequence.

5. **Examine the list.** Decide how your team members will learn the information that is needed in order to be successful with each subcomponent. For example, will they read about the information or will the facilitator present information on the topic to the team? Identify how the understanding of each subcomponent will be assessed by either the team or the facilitator. For example, in some cases, the group can be observed as a way to assess their understanding of a new idea or technique, while in other cases, the

facilitator can ask questions of the group that can be used to assess the members' understanding of the concept.

6. Using all the information generated in relation to the task completion analysis process, **design a plan for how the new tasks or ideas will be integrated into the meeting and learned and used by the team being facilitated.**

The following example illustrates how this works in actual practice:

Sheila was preparing to work as an internal consultant with a group of people in the curriculum division of a school district. She needed to help this group identify the major initiatives for the upcoming school year. In preparing for this meeting, she followed the steps listed above:

1. In Step 1, Sheila had five objectives:

- To develop a completed plan for the curriculum projects for the upcoming year

- To match their plan to the budget they had been allocated

- To learn how to listen to each other with an open mind before drawing conclusions

- To stay on time and stay focused during the meeting

- To make sure everyone understands clearly what the team members agreed to do when they returned to their worksite upon the closure of the meeting

2. In Step 2, Sheila separated the outcomes into two groups: those that were related to the product the group was producing (the plan) and those that related to group meeting skills (see Table 2.6).

3. In Step 3, Sheila listed the components in Table 2.7 for one of the outcomes she identified.

4. In Step 4, since Sheila couldn't see that any particular order needed to be followed for her group to learn about and use these components, she decided to keep the list in the order she had originally listed them. In the meeting she was preparing to facilitate, she decided that she would help her team members learn these components by just taking a few minutes to talk

Table 2.6

Group Product	Group Meeting Process
• Training plan for the year • Match of plan to budget	• Learning how to listen to each other before drawing conclusions • Staying on time and focused • Making sure that everyone understands what the team agreed to do upon returning to work site after the meeting

Table 2.7

Staying on time and focused during the meeting
• Understanding the importance of staying on time and the impact of getting behind on the meeting • Having an awareness of the present time • Being able to accurately estimate the amount of time needed for a discussion time • Understanding the impact of an off-task comment on the group's ability to stay on time with an agenda item

about the issue of staying on time within the guidelines set forth by the agenda. She decided that she would use a wall chart to reinforce the main points to help the group stay on track. Sheila decided to ask the team members at the end of the meeting how these components had impacted their ability to stay on time for the meeting. She would track their responses to assess whether or not the team members had learned about staying on track. She would also keep a log of the group's ability to stay on track as evidence of its completion or lack of completion of this skill.

Breaking up the outcomes as was illustrated in the example can be difficult and cumbersome at first, but soon will become a process that you will be able to complete by thinking through the process rather than having to write down every single step. Given some practice with this concept, the outcomes will be broken down quickly and efficiently. The Outcome Completion Planning Template (Table 2.8) is provided to help with this process.

Table 2.8   Outcome Completion Planning Template

Meeting Outcomes
_____
_____
_____
_____
_____
_____
_____
_____
_____
_____

Task Outcomes	Group Processing Outcomes	Other Pertinent Outcomes

Outcome 1	Outcome 2	Outcome 3	Outcome 4	Outcome 5
Components	Components	Components	Components	Components

PLANNING FOR THE
EFFECTIVE DELIVERY OF DIRECTIONS

Since facilitators rely on the participants to be engaged in activities as a way for them to accomplish the tasks they have been assigned, it is crucial for these facilitators to make sure that the directions they administer are clear and accurate. When working in front of a group facilitating a session, it is common to feel nervous and want to move quickly from one activity to the next. This is where it can be easy to give incomplete or even incoherent directions. Thoroughly planning for this aspect of the facilitation role will minimize the chance of this happening. Keep the following in mind when planning for delivering clear directions:

- Identify the activities in the agenda where multistep, complex directions will need to be delivered. Write down these activities.
- For each activity identified, break it down into the subskills that will need to be accomplished for successful completion of the activity, taking the proper order of the subskills needed to be successful for the activity into consideration.
- Identify the specific information that the participants will need to be given in order to successfully complete each subskill.
- Put the subskills back together into their original form (activity level) and put the directions in the order they need to be given to ensure successful completion of the entire activity.
- Walk through these directions, taking note of any areas that could be confusing or hard to follow. Keep the number of directions to be delivered at one time to a minimum. Identify how the directions will be delivered to the participants.
- Identify the ways that you will check the understanding of the directions by your participants; identify alternate ways you can clarify these directions if misunderstandings occur.
- Jot down in the meeting plans the major points that will need to be addressed in the delivery of these directions; refer to them in the meeting to stay on track.

Use the Direction Delivery Planning Template (Table 2.9) to plan the effective delivery of directions in your meeting.

Table 2.9   Direction Delivery Planning Template

1. What activities in this meeting will need multistep directions to be delivered?

2. What are the subskills needed for each of the areas identified in Step 1 in order for meeting participants to be successful in completing the activities? What specific information will they need to be given in order to complete each of these subskills?

3. How will participants receive the directions? How many directions will they receive at one time (no more than 3-4)?

4. What strategies will be used to check if participants understand the directions you have delivered? What alternate explanations can be used if the initial directions are misunderstood?

SUMMARY

Planning is essential for success in facilitating meetings. Successful facilitators employ a variety of techniques when planning their meetings. This chapter has touched on a few of these ideas and presented practical examples for their use to assist facilitators in implementing them into their practice. Understanding the knowledge base required of facilitators is essential in thinking about planning. The planning checklists provide a starting point for the kinds of components facilitators need to consider in putting together a meeting. The information on agendas, breaking tasks into parts, and planning for the effective delivery of directions are skills that every facilitator can benefit from when working with groups. In Chapter 3, I discuss how to start a session, a key to long-term success with a group. This information will build on the skills and knowledge that have been discussed in this book and add to your professional knowledge base.

Go

What we call results are beginnings.

—Ralph Waldo Emerson

Striving for excellence motivates you; striving for perfection is demoralizing.

—Dr. Harriet Braiker

SETTING THE PROPER TONE FOR A MEETING

Setting a positive tone is very important to a good meeting. A facilitator needs to plan overt activities to establish this positive tone. In their book *Primal Leadership: Realizing the Power of Emotional Intelligence* (2002), authors Daniel Goleman, Richard Boyatzis, and Annie McKee introduce the term "resonance" as it relates to leadership. They point out that in resonance, people are in sync—getting along and working together in a positive manner. Goleman, Boyatzis, and McKee point out that when a group is in the state of resonance, its members feel a mutual comfort level. They share ideas, learn from each other, make decisions collaboratively, and get things done. They form a bond that helps them stay focused even amid profound change and certainty (p. 21).

Resonance transferred to the facilitation experience means that the facilitator works to connect people, that is, to start a meeting with activities and strategies that build a sense of connection and good will. In this chapter, I highlight strategies to create this feeling from the beginning of the meeting. In order to focus your learning as you read this chapter, review the following focusing questions:

- ♦ Why is it important to set a positive tone at the beginning of a meeting?
- ♦ What is the role of framing in keeping a group on track and focused during a meeting?

- How does a foundation-setting activity work to shape the emotions of group members?
- What kinds of music seem to work best to start meetings?
- How do facilitators use ground rules and norms to work with a group and keep them on track?
- What applications from this chapter will fit with my facilitation style and work best with the groups that I facilitate?

Obviously, people remember their first experience in a situation. As the facilitator, how you handle the first few minutes of a meeting is crucial to its success. In Chapter 2, ideas were presented in regard to the planning of a successful meeting. Some of these are

- Designing the physical setup of the room to ensure the comfort of the participants
- Providing refreshments prior to the start of the meeting
- Welcoming participants as they enter the meeting room
- Playing a short, related video clip to start the meeting
- Starting the meeting with a story or short joke
- Playing music in the room as participants enter

All these ideas hold good potential for starting a meeting off on a positive note. The use of music is a powerful way to start a meeting and build the sense of resonance a facilitator needs to get a group on the right track. It is the first area that we will examine in more detail.

THE USE OF MUSIC

One way to set a good tone at the start of a meeting is to use music. As people enter the room, music should be playing lightly in the background. Music appeals to the most basic of human emotions and, when used correctly, can bring people back to positive memories. While the specific kind of music used to start a session depends on the preferences of the facilitator and the group, here are some general guidelines to keep in mind when selecting music for setting a tone in meetings:

- Select music that is motivating and connects emotionally to both the facilitator and the meeting participants. Some facilitators have found that the use of music can help them get emotionally charged up for a meeting.
- Keep the age group or generation of the group in mind as the music is selected. (Many of the people on the teams we facilitate are in the baby boomer generation and tend to be motivated by music of the

1960s and 1970s. Music from so-called light rock stations also works well with these types of groups.)

♦ Consider the lyrics of the songs that are chosen for play. Groups resonate with the lyrics of a familiar song. Songs that have the messages of togetherness, cooperation, and connections in their lyrics communicate subtle messages to a group about an upcoming meeting. These songs also help people reflect back to other positive emotional times in their lives, and they transfer these positive emotions to the upcoming meeting.

♦ Consider the tone needed for the meeting and choose the music that matches this tone. If the group comes to the meeting with a low energy level, consider something upbeat. If the group is charged up and needs to be calmed, consider songs that have a slow tempo; instrumentals can serve this function well.

♦ Use music as a signal to start the meeting or help people make transitions from breaks to activities; announce to team members that the meeting will start at the end of the next song. This helps some members to mentally get prepared for the meeting.

♦ Have fun and experiment with different types of music in starting sessions.

Sources of Music

How do facilitators find good sources of music without having to become disk jockeys? Many good sources are readily available to help in the selection of songs. Most facilitators build up their selection list over time, adding new songs as they encounter them in other situations or become bored with their old standbys. Here are some good sources of a wide variety of music for your facilitation sessions:

♦ Movie sound tracks—especially good for re-creating positive emotions for group members

♦ "Greatest hits" CDs—provide an artist's best songs

♦ "Best of Year" collections—recording industry companies put together songs based on their year of release (these can be good sources of single songs by artists)

♦ Individual artist collections—facilitators can find the original songs on CDs (sometimes good songs can be found that did not make it to the radio. Test these on others before playing them for your meeting)

♦ CD singles—current hits are usually released on CD singles (older hits are usually not available)

♦ EZ listening stations—in addition to using the playlists of these stations to help with the selection of possible songs, some of these stations release remixes of their most popular songs (many of these will have regionally based variations of the most popular songs)

♦ Other facilitators and presenters—many people who conduct workshops have discovered the magic of music and are willing to share their musical secrets with others

♦ Amusement and theme parks—this may seem like an unusual source, but some of the larger corporate properties have the music that is featured in parades and in the ride lines for sale at their gift shops (many of these songs contain good instrumental and lyrical combinations to help energize a group)

♦ Music professionals—music professionals, including musicians and music teachers, have the training and background to help identify and select music sources for specific applications (once a situation is described, they can be quite helpful)

♦ Music store personnel—while they might lack the music theory training of other music professionals, they do listen to the music that is played in the store every day and probably note people's reaction to it (if the type of music desired is described, they can probably direct the interested facilitator to several good selections)

♦ Gift shops—In many gift shops today, music is playing that makes people feel comfortable in purchasing items at the store (ask what is playing; they usually have copies to sell)

♦ Athletic events—certain athletic events have motivating and energizing music playing (for example, I was recently watching some rock climbers working on their technique and started to listen to their motivational music. I asked about the music; they gave me the title, and it has become one of the most popular music selections that I use to start my sessions)

♦ TV commercials and shows—at times, contemporary music is featured in shows and commercials (the TV networks have done a lot of research into what kinds of music motivates people, so it makes sense that these same songs would work to start meetings)

Traditional Music Styles and Their Potential Impact on Group Emotions

While there are many more music styles in the marketplace than are listed here, these represent the major styles that I have used in starting meetings. After each listed style, I have given some information about the impact it has had on a group when used in conjunction with a meeting.

Classical. Can induce a calming effect on group members; can also be used to energize a team, depending on how fast the tempo of the song is. Use recognizable songs to keep the group members from trying to guess what the selection name is as the song is playing.

Country. Has been used with limited success; seems to be geographically based. Groups either love it or don't resonate well with it.

New age. The instrumental versions of this music can be used with success to energize groups. Facilitator will need to preview selections. Choose mainstream new age selections. Be careful when using music that contains lyrics, because some of the words may be objectionable to certain members of your team.

Rock. Songs can be used with careful selection. Soft rock (which has become soft because it is now over 20 years old) can work with groups. Preview selections with representatives before using them with the entire group.

Top 40. Seems to be one of the most popular, especially if the selections are chosen from the eras represented by a majority of the participants. A close examination of the lyrics can identify songs where the lyrics can be used to build an emotional connection as well as the tunes.

Jazz. Tends to build emotional energy. Contains good representation of instruments and has an upbeat tempo. Many baby boomers that attend meetings report to be jazz fans. Many jazz songs do not have lyrics, so they can be used as light background music.

Consider the questions in the Music Use Planning Template (Table 3.1) when planning to use music to start your meetings and at other times in a meeting.

Music is just one way to build group resonance. There are activities that happen right at the beginning of the meeting that can contribute to a collaborative setting. One of those is called a foundation-setting activity.

FOUNDATION-SETTING ACTIVITIES

Another component designed to set a good tone for a meeting is a foundation-setting activity. Foundation-setting activities have the following characteristics.

Foundation-Setting Activities

- ◆ Usually occur at the beginning of a meeting
- ◆ Ask participants to connect with others on the team
- ◆ Utilize familiar or pertinent information
- ◆ Contain an emotional component put into place by the meeting facilitator
- ◆ Set individual expectations for team accomplishments
- ◆ Provide an opportunity to get all group members' voices into the meeting

Table 3.1   Music Use Planning Template

Consider the following questions when planning to use music to start your meetings and at other times in a meeting:

1. What tone needs to be set at the beginning of the meeting in order for the group to be able to think and problem solve together?

    _____
    _____
    _____

2. What are the different generations of people represented on this team? What kinds of music might appeal to their emotional interests?

    _____
    _____
    _____

3. What kind of music appeals to you and would help you generate the kind of energy you need in order to lead this group?

    _____
    _____
    _____

4. List the times you are considering music use:

    *   At the beginning of the meeting
    *   During the meeting at transitional points
    *   As a closure activity at the end of the meeting

5. How do you plan to play the music? Do you need special equipment? Any additional musical selections? What support from others would be beneficial in choosing the music?

    _____
    _____
    _____

Here are some examples of foundation-setting activities:

A facilitator wrote the following directions on a chart tablet that was posted in the front of a room where a meeting was about to occur.

At 9:30 a.m., be ready to share the following:

♦ Your name/role
♦ Something positive that happened in your classroom today
♦ One idea you hope to gain as a result of today's meeting

This foundation-setting activity contains the components necessary to shape the emotions of the group, connect members together, and set an expectation for the learning of the team members. In this example, the facilitator chose to have each of the members share their answers to the prompts individually because of the small size of the group. In large groups, it might be better to have people form small clusters, pairs, or trios for the sharing to make the activity more time efficient.

In another example, Steve, the meeting facilitator, said the following at the beginning of a meeting he was facilitating:

"Today, we will start our meeting with a brief opening. This opening is designed to give us more information about each other that we will need to know as we work together. Take 30 seconds and jot down your responses to the following:

♦ Share something about yourself that very few others in the room would know.
♦ Talk about a success you've had in the last 2 weeks in your personal or professional life.
♦ Discuss what you would like to accomplish as a result of this meeting and how you will work to make that desire happen."

As you can see, this foundation-setting activity is slightly different from the first example. In this case, because Steve knew that group members had worked together for a period of time, the activity in the first example would not be appropriate for Steve's group. He is moving participants to a deeper personal knowledge level when he asks them to share something about themselves that few other people in the room would know. It's up to each participant to decide the personal story that will be shared within the group. Many times group participants are surprised at what they learn about their colleagues as a result of an opening such as this.

In a third example, Teri uses a foundation-setting activity in a different manner to start a group. In this situation, a task force was formed to study a new curricular program. This program was controversial. Teri knew that many of the members had negative feelings and emotions that they had brought to the meeting with them. She also knew that if these negative feelings were not brought to the table, they would hinder the group's decision-making progress during the meeting. She designed the foundation-setting activity to allow some of these negative feelings to be released in a controlled manner.

> As people entered the room for the curriculum meeting, she wrote the following on a piece of chart paper:
>
> At 7:30 P.M., be ready to
>
> ♦ Introduce yourself and share your role in the district and on this team.
> ♦ Share a positive experience you've had with one aspect of our school curriculum over the last couple of years.
> ♦ Discuss your greatest fear associated with this new curricular program.
>
> (We'll be talking about your ideas and concerns as we move through the meeting.)

In this session, Teri stood at a chart and wrote down people's fears without making any comments as they shared them. Once all fears were listed, Teri used this chart as a teaching tool for the group. She asked group members to look over the chart and identify the general trends they noticed in the concerns. She had the participants meet in groups of three to discuss these trends and their danger to the new curricular program. Finally, she had these groups of three generate strategies to overcome these fears. This was a very productive exercise for this task force because they were able to openly present problems but were also able to generate possible solutions for these areas. In the opening section of the meeting, the group was able to solve about a third of the concerns that were expressed. Teri posted the chart of concerns in front of the room so the members could scan it during the meeting. By the end of the meeting, about two thirds of the concerns had been addressed by the group.

Foundation-setting activities help set a positive tone for the beginning of the meeting. In addition, they can be used to gather important information, as was illustrated in the examples. Even though most foundation-setting activities take place at the beginning of the meeting, the strategy can be used at any time when the facilitator feels the group is becoming disconnected. Here are two examples where some components of the strategy are employed during a meeting with a difficult group when the facilitator feels the group needs a moment to reenergize.

1. In working with a team whose job it was to evaluate the school improvement plan for their site and make recommendations for new initiatives, Michelle noticed that two factions were forming within this team. She could tell that people were getting angry with each other. She decided it was time to stop the discussion and set a new foundation for the group. As the group finished its discussion, she stepped off to the side and wrote the following directions on chart paper:

Take a minute to respond to the following ideas:

♦ Specifically, what progress has our group made today in relation to the school improvement process?
♦ What communication difficulties seem to be inhibiting us from making further progress?
♦ How do we overcome these difficulties in order to move forward?

Michelle told the participants that they were getting stuck on one component of the school improvement plan and needed to take a moment to refine their thoughts. She turned the chart toward the group and asked group members to stand and talk with a partner about the three questions she had posted. She allowed each pair to share their ideas with the entire group. She wrote down their responses to Question 3 and helped the group come to consensus on the strategies they would use to keep their communication channels open. Whenever the group began to experience difficulties in communication, Michelle referred them back to the chart and reminded them of their agreement to continue an open discussion.

2. After about an hour of talking about its strategic plan for the upcoming year, a team that Stan was facilitating seemed to be getting tired. Stan decided to give them a 10-minute break. Before the group members were dismissed for the break, Stan asked them to come back and be ready to talk about two issues: the amount of progress they had made on the plan and what they had left to address.

After the break, Stan had put the two prompts on a piece of chart paper and started by asking members to meet in trios to talk about the ideas on the chart. As Stan walked around, he could sense an increase in the energy of the group. When he asked the group members to share their thoughts, they had many good ideas that they were interested in contributing. Once he reengaged them in the strategic planning discussion, they finished in a short time. Several of the participants commented on how helpful it was for them to meet in the small groups to talk about their progress and ideas for what components were left to address.

In this example, Stan used a foundation-setting activity in a slightly different way than was illustrated in the other examples in this chapter. He combined the strategy with a break to help his team members use the break time to think about how they needed to complete the strategic plan. The use of a break as a thinking and problem-solving opportunity can be a good use of the time. In this case, the group members thought that they were taking a break, but in addition to getting up and moving around a little, they were also thinking. The foundation-setting activity Stan had them complete upon returning from break was just the thing they needed to get their creative energy moving again.

Foundation-setting activities can be highly effective icebreakers to start a meeting. Use the template in Table 3.2 to plan for the foundation-setting activities you would like to use in your next meeting.

Foundation-setting activities have a certain pattern that is typically used in their generation that structures the group's response to them. Another opening activity that is closely related to foundation-setting activities is an opener called Good News. Its structure is slightly different, but it can be just as effective in working with a team.

GOOD NEWS

In this opener, participants are asked to talk about something good that has happened to them since the last time the group met. The examples can be personal or professional, and are usually brief in nature. This type of opener has the effect of helping to start the meeting off in a positive manner, but it also provides information that team members can use to get to know a little more about each other. It builds resonance because of the collegiality and familiarity that is apparent after the examples are shared. Team members start to say things like "I didn't know . . . " or " . . . and I have something in common." I have used the Good News strategy extensively

Table 3.2   Foundation-Setting Activities Planning Template

1. What kinds of emotional issues do your team members typically bring to your meeting? How do you think foundation-setting activities could positively shape the emotions of your group?

    _____

    _____

    _____

2. What kinds of familiar content or topics could the group use in starting the foundation-setting activity?

    _____

    _____

    _____

3. Write down some statements you could use to help the team you are facilitating to generate positive examples to share with the group. Consider using classroom-related prompts, positive happenings from their personal lives, or stories that illustrate positive impacts of others.

    _____

    _____

    _____

4. What kinds of personal commitments to the group success or desired outcomes for the meeting do you want them to generate as a part of the last prompt of the foundation-setting activity? How can it be shaped so it is stated in a positive manner?

    _____

    _____

    _____

5. How will the information provided to you be captured? What parts of their foundation-setting activity might come in handy for future reference?

    _____

    _____

    _____

and found that groups have actually looked forward to it in meetings. Some examples of prompts that you might consider using to start a meeting include the following:

- ◆ "Share something good that has happened to you since our last time together."
- ◆ "What ideas have you thought about in relation to our task since our last meeting?"
- ◆ "Share something that has been good news to you since we last met."
- ◆ "Talk about a positive that you have experienced as a result of being on this team."
- ◆ "Find a partner and talk about something good that happened to you this week."
- ◆ "Think about a situation where you have recently encountered something that was potentially negative, but through your efforts, it became positive."
- ◆ "Share an example of someone you know who helps to make your day when you see that person."

Ideas to Keep in Mind When Using Good News

- ◆ Be sure that during your first attempts in using this strategy, you have talked with people in advance who will be ready to share a good news item with the group.
- ◆ Build in Good News as an agenda item with its own time and place on the agenda. If you don't, it could be left off or neglected.
- ◆ When introducing the concept, be sure to explain how it will help the group to function better as a team. Let group members know that you are purposely using the Good News idea to help meetings be more productive.
- ◆ After asking for Good News ideas, be sure to pause and wait for people to share their stories. Because group members may be shy or reluctant to share right away, it may take a few minutes for the positive stories to surface. If you move on too quickly, you will negatively reinforce participation, resulting in the strategy not working for your team.
- ◆ As you use the Good News strategy in future meetings, be sure to ask a variety of people to start by sharing their Good News items so that the same team members do not always have to carry the positiveness of the entire group.
- ◆ As group members bring up positive examples, and at the end of the Good News session, be sure to reinforce them for their efforts. Make sure that you are sincere in your praise so that they will continue to participate in Good News sessions in the future.

If used properly and consistently, Good News can become a valuable part of regular meetings and something that people look forward to as they become more comfortable in self-disclosing to others on their team.

THE USE OF FRAMING

An effective tool to help set a good tone at the start of a meeting and to help shape the discussion in a meeting is framing. In framing, the facilitator sets the boundaries for the session and the discussion that will occur in the meeting. The facilitator draws a verbal boundary around the discussion or session. The facilitator also assumes some control over the group by setting the boundaries for the discussion. The following framing statement examples should provide some clarity in regard to this strategy:

1. As we work together today, we need to make sure that our discussion focuses on ideas that we will want to consider for our employee recognition program."

2. "I know that some of you are interested in finding out where the potential budget cuts will be, but we will need to focus on our task, which is helping to identify potential income sources. At the end of the meeting, I'd be happy to meet with the group to share the budget cut information that I am aware of at this point."

3. "Our group keeps getting off track because we are looking at the obstacles to our work. What we need to focus on right now are the potential benefits of what we are doing. At the end of the night, we can look at those issues that will hinder our progress."

In all these examples, the facilitator used verbal statements to draw a boundary around the discussion of the group that was being facilitated. In framing, the facilitator is able to keep the group on track through the statement. Framing not only depends on the credibility of the facilitator, but it builds the credibility of the facilitator because the group sees the level of control exerted by this person. In the Garmston and Wellman (1999) set of facilitator skills discussed in Chapter 2, framing would fit best under the area of facilitator moves, because frames tend to be delivered in response to the group getting off task. Some facilitators plan their frames in advance and deliver them before the group is moving off task, so in this case a frame might be considered a strategy in the Garmston and Wellman model. In either case, frames are highly effective. The following considerations need to be kept in mind in reference to framing.

Considerations for Framing
Statements at the Beginning of a Meeting

◆ Start using framing as a strategy that will be incorporated in the beginning of a meeting.

◆ Think about the perspectives that the participants will be bringing to the meeting. Try to imagine what distractions from the posted agenda content could take them off track.

◆ Plan an opening that sets the parameters for the meeting. Design statements that will establish these parameters, such as

  ◆ "Today we are here to talk about . . . "
  ◆ "The major points we need to address are . . . "
  ◆ "As we work together we need to . . . "
  ◆ "Even though there are other new topics that could be addressed in our meeting, we need to focus on . . . "
  ◆ "At our last meeting, we got off track because of . . . In this meeting, we need to get . . . "
  ◆ "Since we have limited time and personal energy, we are going to make sure that we stay on . . . "

◆ As you deliver the framing statement, be sure to stand still and look at the participants. This allows you to focus on their reactions to the statement. Make note of their reactions; use them for future reference or connect with those participants who seem to have a particularly negative reaction at a break.

◆ Consider using a hand gesture that signifies focus in conjunction with your statement. People perceive body language very accurately and subconsciously. For example, if your framing statement involves asking the group to narrow its focus, hold your hands to signify narrowing. Gestures will reinforce your verbal statements.

Framing Statement Examples

The following examples provide additional ways that framing can be used at the start of a meeting to constrain the discussion topics:

1. "I know that several of you would like to talk about the news report from last night on our organization, but we have very limited time to accomplish the task we have been assigned, so we need to stay on task for today's meeting."

2. "I know that several of you would like to talk about the news report from last night on our organization, but we have very limited time to accomplish the task we have been assigned. If we can get

finished with our agenda in a timely fashion, we can take some time to talk about the situation at the end of our meeting."

3. "I know that several of you would like to talk about the news report from last night on our organization, but we have very limited time to accomplish the task we have been assigned. Since the issue is so important, lets take the first 10 minutes of our meeting today to clarify the issues of the news report. We'll need to move along on our original agenda more quickly."

Each of these examples is based on the same incident. During the pre-meeting time, when participants were arriving, the facilitator overheard several team members talking about a situation where the organization was featured on the local news for some labor problems it was experiencing. Several members of the team had talked to the facilitator about having some time to talk about this issue at the upcoming meeting. Each of the responses listed above reflects the degree to which the facilitator felt that the issue needed to be discussed. In Example 1, the facilitator didn't allow time for the discussion to occur. In Example 2, the facilitator decided that the issue was important, but not important enough to be placed in front of other more pressing issues. Finally, in Example 3, the facilitator obviously thought that the issue was important to many of the team members. He placed it at the start of the agenda so that the issue could be put to rest and the team could go on with its business. He constrained the time allocated for the discussion, however, so that other business could still be accomplished.

ACTIVE LEARNING STRATEGIES

The beginning of a facilitative session is a good time to get group members engaged and connected in the meeting by providing active learning activities. Not only is participation more interesting than just sitting down and listening, but it also serves to engage and energize people. Implementing active learning activities at the beginning of a meeting sets the tone for the expectation of engagement for the entire meeting. While there are many active learning strategies that could be used with a group, choose those that are simple and easy to implement. It diminishes the tone if members are confused and irritated by a complicated opening activity. Here are some that are simple for the group to follow:

♦ Ask your group members to stand and talk with another person about their day; ask them to share some of the positive aspects of their day.

♦ Pair people up and ask them to talk about the agenda that has been provided for this session. Have these pairs discuss what they think will come out of the meeting today.

♦ Have group members turn to the person next to them and talk about the first few items on the agenda. Have them share how they think the group can accomplish their goals in a positive way.

♦ Ask team members to jot down one or two ideas that they hope the group gets to talk about in the meeting today. Have them share these in groups of three or four.

♦ Give the group members a copy of the agenda, ask them to look it over and discuss it in pairs, talking about how they see each item impacting the overall mission of the team or committee.

Active learning doesn't necessarily mean that the group is getting up and jumping around the room; it refers to the engagement of their minds (and bodies) in the activity. Active learning can involve much more than was illustrated here, but it can also be fairly low key in nature. Simple and direct activities work much better than complex participation strategies. By engaging the group in some type of active strategy at the beginning of the meeting, it gets members thinking and connected right away. It can be better for their involvement than what normally happens when they come to a meeting—they get to sit and listen to someone talk to them. By using some form of activity in the opening minutes, it is possible to throw members a curve ball that they aren't expecting. This novelty can hook them from the start and keep them engaged during the entire meeting.

WATCHING TEAM MEMBER BEHAVIORS DURING THE START OF A MEETING

The first few minutes of a meeting provide the facilitator the opportunity to watch a team and see how they participate and interact. Normally, people will be a little subdued during the start of a meeting, so this needs to be taken into consideration when observing the group. Here are some points to consider when watching a group to gauge their interaction during the start of a meeting.

Opening Group Behavior Considerations

♦ Watch people as they enter the room. You should be able to easily spot those who seem like they might be ready to work and those who may need some additional attention to stay focused during your session together.

♦ As the members mingle around waiting for the meeting to get started, be sure to see which people are talking and which people are avoiding each other. This can give you important information that you can use later in assigning partners and figuring out why small teams are not being effective in their operation.

♦ Watch for body language indicators that let you know everything is fine or that a problem is brewing. If people are engaged, animated, and appear relaxed, you are probably going to have a productive meeting. If, on the other hand, you notice that they are exhibiting defensive or unwelcoming body language, look out.

♦ Pay particular attention to people as you conduct the opening activities. If they readily participate, you should have a productive meeting; if they openly resist or refuse to participate, it could be an indication of trouble ahead for you and this group

OPENING THE SESSION

Since people make their judgments about others in the first few minutes of an interaction, it is crucial to open the session as positively as possible. Here are several things to keep in mind as you open a facilitation session with several kinds of groups.

Opening a Session With a Group That You Are Familiar With

While it might sound like this would be an easy situation to deal with, opening a session with familiar people can be challenging for some. Since they already know you, they tend to have preconceived notions about you and your meeting. Here are some points to consider when opening up a meeting with this type of group:

♦ Be sure to welcome the group and thank them for giving their time to this meeting. Be sincere and honest in your comments. Group members can see right through fake or phony opening compliments.

♦ Remind the group of any past accomplishments or progress they have made in working on this topic. If they have not addressed these issues, provide them with a short background of the topic area.

♦ Be sure to talk about the agenda that has been developed for this meeting, any background in relation to its development, and any inside issues they need to be aware of in working on this area. Remind the group members of any ground rules or operating procedures that they have been operating under in past meetings.

♦ Using positive presuppositions, let the group members know of your optimism about their future work with statements such as "Even though this work will take time, I know that together we can do it" or "We haven't been able to make as much progress on our task as we would have liked in the past, but today we will make some significant decisions."

♦ Reinforce any expertise or experiences in the group that may contribute to its success with the process.

Opening a Session With an Unfamiliar Group

Opening a session with a group that you have not worked with before also has its own challenges. With an unfamiliar group, you may need to work during your first session to establish credibility with them as their facilitator. Keep the following in mind as you work with these kinds of groups:

♦ Welcome the group to the meeting; thank them for their time and energy in helping to address the issue at hand.

♦ Give them a thumbnail sketch of your background and experience. It is important for them to know that you have expertise in working with groups. Don't go overboard with this introduction, but be sure to address the important points that may match the needs of the group. If you have worked with curriculum committees in the past, let then know that fact if this group is making a curricular decision. This helps them to understand why you were selected to work with their team.

♦ Set or draw out the group ground rules that will govern the operation of the meeting.

♦ Go over the agenda and discuss any logistical elements, such as the timing of breaks, the location of restrooms, or anything else that the group will need to know to function productively.

♦ Use presuppositions to help set the tone for the meeting. Statements like those contained in the example above may help the group to stay on track as they meet together.

♦ Be sure to check and see if there are any special needs in the group. You may find that one of your group members needs to be seated toward the front or may have some other physical issue that prevents him or her from participating fully in the meeting. It is better to know this up front rather than offending the group later in the meeting. Use sensitivity in asking for this information. Since people have varying levels of comfort with these issues, be looking for a nonobtrusive way to find out this information.

SETTING NORMS AND GROUND RULES

In starting and conducting meetings with groups, it is very important to operate under ground rules or norms. These items provide the structure for the meeting to be operated in a positive, constructive manner. Group norms relate to the behaviors that the group has agreed to follow in working together. They are included in this chapter on starting meetings because they provide an important foundation for group success. The group has developed ownership in the norms. Ground rules, on the other hand, are parameters that the facilitator has set for the team interactions. They are used with groups that have not yet set norms, groups that meet too infrequently to build the kind of working relationship to set norms, or with groups incapable of setting their own norms. Ground rules are important foundationally for group success as well.

Norms

The following is a list of some of the possible norms that teams use in order to direct their work and their meeting procedures.

Sample Norms of Productive Teams or Groups

♦ Use active listening strategies while members share ideas.
♦ Come to meetings ready to learn and work.
♦ Try to understand other group members' perspectives on issues.
♦ Leave your negative emotions at the door.
♦ Presume that all group members are trying to do their best.
♦ During brainstorming activities, do not judge the contributions.
♦ Practice suspending your opinion temporarily when you hear an idea you initially disagree with.
♦ Make sure that everyone has an equal chance to participate.
♦ When a new idea is shared, do not agree or disagree too quickly.
♦ Honor time limits and commitments.
♦ Always look at the pros and cons of an issue.
♦ Work to preserve the equal status of all members on this team.
♦ Understand and mediate the influence you and your comments have on others in this group.
♦ Continue to work toward community.
♦ Always get more details on an idea or issue before making a final decision.
♦ Use reflective paraphrases to help other team members know that you understand the points they are making.
♦ When asking a clarifying question, be sure that it is open ended and nonjudgmental in nature.

♦ If you do not understand a suggestion or the information another team member has given you, probe deeper through the use of clarifying questions.

♦ Always check to see if everyone is in agreement before moving on with an issue.

♦ Follow the agreements made within the group when communicating with those not on this committee.

♦ Come to sessions with an open mind, ready to try new things and learn from each other.

These and other norms that groups develop are essential in the decision-making process. Without norms, groups can have great difficulty in staying true to the processes that help them be more productive as a team. While norms tend to be set by the decision-making team, ground rules are more likely to be set by the person facilitating the meeting. Let's take a look at the concept of ground rules and how they could be helpful to team operation.

Ground Rules

Ground rules are the parameters that are set by the person facilitating a meeting in order to ensure the productive operation of a team. They are very similar to norms but don't have the team ownership that norms do and can be harder to enforce than norms. Here are some examples of ground rules:

Sample Ground Rules

♦ "Listen as others speak."

♦ "We will not move forward until everyone has had a chance to share an idea."

♦ "During our dialogue, there will be no sidebar discussions."

♦ "Only one person at a time can talk."

♦ "When we call a vote, everyone must indicate a preference."

♦ "What is discussed in this meeting stays in this meeting unless agreed upon by all members of the team."

♦ "All ideas will be written down on the chart paper before they are to be considered by the group."

♦ "There will be no name calling or put-downs in this meeting."

♦ "As we discuss the main issues, you can't blame another person or group in the room for the problems in the system."

♦ "Some members are only here as observers; they have no final decision-making vote."

♦ "Once the meeting has started, we will take turns in commenting on the ideas presented by the group."

Ground rules are more directive in nature than are norms. Either norms or ground rules are an essential part of the initial operation of an effective team and are strategies that should be implemented by facilitators.

SUMMARY

Strategies for starting an effective meeting are discussed in this chapter. Music has a way of hooking into the positive emotions of participants and helping connect them to the meeting. Framing statements can keep a group focused on their proposed agenda items and help them have a productive meeting. The role of norms and ground rules are discussed in this chapter as well as ideas for starting meetings with both familiar and unfamiliar groups. All of the ideas in this chapter, if used effectively, will help set the tone of the meeting and make the experience both pleasurable and productive for the participants and the facilitator as they work together to accomplish their assigned tasks.

Now that the meeting is under way, it will be important to help the group work together in an interdependent manner. In Chapter 4, "Connecting All Members of the Team," I discuss strategies to help team members work as a combined, connected unit.

Connecting
All Members
of the Team

Give a man a fish, you feed him for a day; teach him how to fish, you feed him for a lifetime.

—Lao-tzu

We need to listen to one another if we are to make it through this age of apocalypse and avoid the chaos of the crowd.

—Chaim Potok

Team membership is at the core of human needs. People naturally want to work together. If this is so, why do so many teams experience difficulty in working together? This chapter is designed to provide practical strategies to connect team members and build a sense of interdependence. Review the following focusing questions to help guide your learning as you read through this chapter:

- What is the importance of building community with teams?
- What stages do groups go through as they become a community?
- What activities seem to promote the sense of community?
- How do communities deal with conflict?

INTERDEPENDENCE/COMMUNITY AND ITS IMPORTANCE TO TEAM OPERATION

A team or group of people can be a dynamic force that presents challenges not unlike a family. People on the team have certain roles they feel they must fulfill, team members can have disagreements with each other, and misunderstandings can occur. We bring people together and hope to draw out their diverse perspectives in order to broaden the scope of the solutions that our group is able to develop as a part of their working together.

When a group is operating in an interdependent manner, it is working together for the good of the group while maintaining the identities of the individuals on the team. This blend of individual and team creates a condition that many change agents call synergy. In general, groups operating as interdependent teams share several of the following characteristics.

Characteristics of Interdependent Teams

♦ A sense of belonging to a group while keeping the members' own unique identities

♦ An appreciation for the unique talents and ideas brought to the table by each member

♦ The understanding of the importance of group norms and operating procedures

♦ The ability to engage in dialogue that expands the members' understanding of others and their ideas rather than engaging in debates and discussion

♦ The feeling that everyone's ideas in a group have merit for consideration

♦ The use of consensus procedures in decision making

♦ The ability to support each other as the group is going through chaos

Examples of Interdependent Teams in Action

Although each team may operate differently while working in an interdependent situation, here are some examples of teams that are exhibiting interdependent characteristics:

1. As a group gets ready to brainstorm ideas for a major decision on parent-teacher conferences, the facilitator, Bill, reminds the members to listen to all the ideas shared by group members before drawing conclusions or making judgments. As ideas are shared,

one member of the group writes them down. At the end of the sharing session, group members ask open-ended clarification questions before deciding which of the ideas to keep and which to eliminate. All member ideas are judged on their merit in the greater scope of the decision.

2. When this team was first called together to work on the school improvement plan, Kim took some time to allow members a chance to get to know each other and understand the strengths that each member brought to the team. As the team begins to encounter some minor difficulties, the members know that they can divide up the work so that each person is working within his or her area of strength. For example, some members are more detail oriented than others, so they work on gathering and interpreting student achievement data. Other members are more global in their orientation, so they work to develop the communications that will be sent to the school-community partners. A third group understands how to develop effective presentations, so that group is put in charge of designing the data presentations that will be given to the community. Once these preliminary projects are put together, the entire team examines the work to make sure it still is in line with the vision established by this group for the school improvement process.

3. A site-based decision-making council understands the importance of communication with the group it represents. The members make an effort to develop an effective communication process. At the beginning of a typical meeting, each of the members reports on the comments that he or she has received during the last month. The team takes the time to try and understand the nature of the communication and how it impacts the operation of this group. This use of communication keeps the group connected to the larger group that it represents.

In these examples, the productive behaviors aren't much different from what would be expected from a lot of teams. The behaviors illustrated here don't necessarily make these group members interdependent; it is how they integrate these behaviors into the greater scope of their work that makes them interdependent. These teams make an overt effort to manage their relationships in this manner. Interdependent teams have a blend of independence and team that works together to make them highly effective in their operation. Team members understand their unique strengths as well as the strengths of the entire group. The blend of self and team makes these groups effective.

What happens to groups as they work together in this kind of atmosphere? How do they form such tight working relationships? Let's look at the impact of community on team operation.

COMMUNITY

There are several models of community that groups use to help gauge their progress in developing this concept. One that has proved useful to many groups is based on the work of M. Scott Peck. In his book *The Different Drum* (1987), Peck highlights the following four stages that teams normally progress through in their quest for community.

1. Pseudocommunity

Peck describes the first stage of group formation as pseudocommunity. In this stage the group normally experiences the following:

- There is little interpersonal connection between members.
- Conflict in the group is not addressed in a productive manner.
- A small number of the group members control the group.
- When members are together, they "fake" connected relationships; members behave in a "cocktail party" mode.
- People in a group speak in very general terms. When pushed to specifics, some members openly resist.
- Since the connections between members is weak, they address their problems behind the backs of others on their team.

2. Chaos

In almost every team's existence, there comes a time when the group experiences a situation or series of situations where the circumstances are out of its direct control. These can be major or minor in nature, but can have either a positive or negative impact on the operation of the team and the relationships of the members. Here are some additional impacts of chaos:

- The group is involved with some type of conflict that causes it to appear out of control.
- An adverse condition comes to a team that requires some type of change on its part in order to reestablish equilibrium.
- The circumstances surrounding the team are out of its direct control.

◆ When members are experiencing this loss of control, there is a desire by at least some group members to quickly get the situation back into control and return to the "good old days."

◆ Because of the loss of control, team members may take out their emotions on each other.

3. Emptiness

Peck explains this stage by calling it a bridge between chaos and community. In the emptiness stage, group members have emerged from chaos and shed the baggage that they held in pseudocommunity and discovered in chaos. Emptiness has the following characteristics in a group:

◆ The members have chosen to let go of the prejudices, predispositions, and other negative emotions that have built up between them during their time together or as a result of previous interactions.

◆ The group members become open to understanding and accepting the differences between members; they begin to see these differences as important to their success as a team.

◆ Rather than revisiting issues that have plagued the group in the past, members decide to move forward, reconciling those items that can be reconciled and dropping those items where a permanent difference of opinion will continue to exist. Members in the last category agree to disagree.

4. Community

The final group stage and the one that Peck contends is the highest level of operation is community. When a group is in true community, it is working together in an interdependent manner to make decisions, implement ideas, and support the entire school community. There are several other characteristics about community to keep in mind:

◆ People in a group that is in community are open to new learning and using the expertise of group members to solve problems.

◆ Teams have well-developed processes to nurture and use diversity to expand the range of possibilities.

◆ Group members use suspension of opinion to allow them to listen to and consider the contributions offered by others.

◆ There is a sense that the whole is greater than the sum of the parts; the concept of synergy is present.

◆ Group members work in a resonant or collaborative environment rather than one of dissonance or lack of harmony.

The team members are able to work through tough issues, tackle difficult problems, and openly deal with conflict but still maintain a connected atmosphere because of their ability to separate an issue from a personality.

TEAM BUILDING

Working toward community is a desired result for teams, but it is not a process that just happens naturally; facilitators need to consider team-building activities to be implemented with the groups they facilitate. Many team members may have a negative connotation of team building. Those feelings may be the result of the following:

- ♦ Participants feel a lack of connection between their previous team-building experiences and real content or situations they may face.
- ♦ Previous team-building activities may not have been debriefed to help participants apply their skills to related situations.
- ♦ Some facilitators may have diminished team building by making a joke out of previous efforts.
- ♦ Previous efforts may have been too hurried for proper learning to occur.

These and other issues can work against attempts to connect group members together with team-building activities. There are a multitude of activities that can be used to help group members work together and move toward a sense of community. When selecting team building, consider these major points:

- ♦ Initially, select activities that are simple to explain and conduct; build in more complexity as you and your group gain confidence.
- ♦ Consider the group members you are working with and what they like to do. Select activities that seem to match their learning and processing strengths.
- ♦ Make sure that the activities you choose can be tied to actual content or situations your team is actually encountering.
- ♦ Keep the team-building activity moving forward as efficiently as possible. Once you begin to detect lowered emotional energy, move to something else.
- ♦ Before introducing an activity to the group, think through the directions carefully in order to minimize confusion.
- ♦ Select activities that you can debrief to help your group transfer what the members of the team you are working with have learned in the activity to other situations they will face.

Physical Versus Mental Team-Building Activities

Both mental and physical team-building activities can help a team to work together toward community. In physical team building, group members are actually engaged in performing a task that is physical in nature, while in mental team building, the individuals engage their thinking processes. In the sample activities listed here, the mental and physical attributes are highlighted.

Physical Team-Building Strategy: Toxic Waste Transfer

The toxic waste transfer task requires the group members to transport objects across an open space without directly touching the objects or their container. The group will manipulate a bucket filled with small objects using ropes attached to the bucket.

Description. The group members form a circle around a 5-gallon bucket. This bucket has numerous ropes attached to it. The group members must hold on to the end of the ropes. Working together, the group will transport the bucket from one spot to another by manipulating the ropes. The group will also use these ropes to transfer the contents of the bucket to another container. In either transporting or transferring the waste, if any of it spills, the members must elect a waste cleanup specialist who will clean up the waste. The group must then go back to the beginning and start the process over again.

Equipment. In order to complete this task, you will need to make a toxic waste transfer bucket. Take an empty 5-gallon bucket, drill between 15 and 20 small holes randomly in the sides. Thread ropes of at least 8 feet in length through the holes, tying a knot on the inside end of each rope. For the toxic waste, fill the bucket with tennis balls, golf balls, Styrofoam peanuts, or other material that can be poured in an efficient manner. Your bucket should look like Figure 4.1.

Procedure

Place the bucket in one location approximately 50 to 60 feet from another container that will hold the entire contents of the original bucket. Discuss the following rules with your group:

◆ The group can use only the ropes to move and transfer the waste. If a group member touches the bucket or the waste, the group must go back to the beginning and start over.
◆ Once the bucket is picked up by the group, it cannot be set down until the waste is transferred.

Figure 4.1

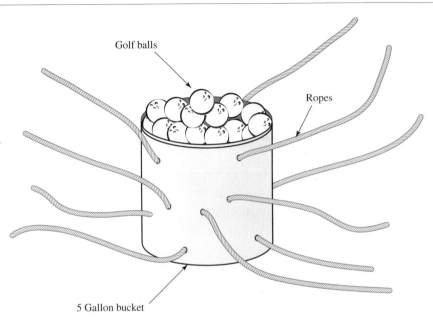

If any waste spills in the movement or transfer process, the group must select a waste cleanup specialist, put all the waste back into the original bucket, and start the process from the beginning.
- Each rope on the bucket must have a person on it, and each person on the team must be touching a rope.
- Team members cannot be any closer to the bucket than half the length of the rope.

Conclusion of the Task. The task is concluded when all the material has been transferred from the original container to the second container. The facilitator needs to debrief the activity by asking team members to talk about what they learned about each other and the team as a result of this activity.

(From *More Team Building Challenges*, by Daniel Midura and Donald Glover, 1995).

Mental Team-Building Activity: The Great Communicator

The Great Communicator is an important activity for helping to build a team. This activity builds communication skills between group members. It emphasizes the importance of speaking and listening. This challenge can be done with limited space and materials.

Description. The team members can sit in either a semicircle or randomly in an area. One member of the group is selected as the Great

Communicator. This person stands in front of the group. The Great Communicator attempts to describe a picture in terms that will allow group members to draw the objects being described. This person may not, however, use certain terms describing standard shapes such as circle, square, rectangle, or triangle. The group may not ask the Great Communicator any questions or request further descriptions.

Equipment. Each group member will need a pencil and one piece of paper per drawing. Each Great Communicator will need a relatively simple picture to describe. A clipboard should be used by the Great Communicator so that group members cannot see through the paper and copy the drawing.

Conclusion of the Task. Once the picture has been fully described, the activity is over. Group members will then share the products of their drawings with each other. The sharing of the drawing can promote some fun and interesting discussions between team members. This on its own can be something that will promote community in itself. Members in this activity tend to laugh, comment on each other's drawing, and have fun with it in general.

(From *More Team Building Challenges,* by Daniel Midura and Donald Glover, 1995)

Physical Team Building: All Tied Up

This physical challenge helps to make participants aware of the difficulty associated with nonverbal communication and helps them to be more in sync with their problem-solving skills. It provides a group the opportunity to work on its collaborative problem-solving skills and learn how to develop alternative communication skills besides verbal or linguistic skills.

Description. Group members are placed in a single file line and asked to hold on to a rope that is about 100 feet long. This rope has between 10 and 12 knots tied in it at equal lengths along its distance. Each group member must hold on to the rope with one hand. The object of the activity is to have the group get all the knots out of the rope while the members are still holding on to the rope. Group members can all face the same direction or they can face in different directions. The important thing to remember is that group members must not let go of the rope in accomplishing the task. Group members cannot talk during the task.

Equipment. For this activity, you will need a soft rope that is about ½ inch in diameter and 100 feet long. You will need to tie 10 to 12 loose knots equally spaced along the length of the rope. The group will need to do the activity in a room that is large enough for the group to have enough space to spread out a little in order to be able to move around when untying the knots. The length of rope here is perfect for a group of about a dozen people. For large groups, divide them into smaller teams and provide them a private space to do the activity.

Conclusion of the Task. Once all the knots are out of the rope, the activity is finished. Since members cannot let go of the rope to untie it, they will need to enlarge the knots and pass their body through them. After the rope is free, engage the team members in a dialogue about the activity and what they learned as a result of the process. Be sure to have them talk about how the dynamics were shaped by the fact that they were unable to verbally communicate during the activity.

Mental Team-Building Activity: Building a Winning Hand

This simple but effective team-building activity gets people to mingle, connect with others, and learn more about each other. It can be implemented with medium to large groups.

Description. In this team-building exercise, members are given 5 playing cards from a standard 52-card deck. The team members are asked to gain information from other team members by asking them questions. As they interact with the other team members, they try to get cards from them that will help them build a winning poker hand. The group members gain cards by trading with other group members as they hold discussions. The person with the highest hand at the end of a short time period is declared the winner. Each time they interact with a person, they can pick only one card. It may take several rounds for them to collect a good hand.

Equipment. In order to do this activity, you will need cards from a standard playing deck and a set of questions to ask other team members. If the group is large, you may need to use two decks to make sure everyone gets five cards; if the group is on the small side, you may need to give members more than five cards.

Some sample information you may have team members obtain could include the following:

♦ Find out what made them interested in getting into education.
♦ Ask members to share a funny story about a recent interaction they have had with children.
♦ Let the group members share an interesting hobby.
♦ Ask people to share their educational background.
♦ Have members describe their favorite relaxation activity.

As you plan for your group, select topics that will let team members learn interesting and helpful information about their peers that will also contribute to the working relationships of the group. Be sure to think about ideas that will be meaningful and accepted by the group. Be careful in the initial stages about getting too personal too fast.

Conclusion of the Task. At the end of a reasonable amount of time, stop the activity, clarify the winning order of poker hands (i.e., royal flush, straight flush, four of a kind, full house, straight, three of a kind, two pair, one pair), and ask members to share their hands with the group. Involve the group in determining the winning hand or hands. Provide some type of simple prize at the end for the winner. Thank the group members for their participation. Have the members debrief the activity, highlighting what they have learned about their peers and the team as a result of this activity. Ask them to share how they can use this information as they continue to work together in the future. Periodically refer to what they have learned in this activity as they work together in the future.

(Adapted from *The Big Book of Team Building Games*, by John Newstrom and Edward Scannel, 1998)

Mental Team-Building Activity: Add a Word

In this team-building activity, group members learn about the value of bringing lots of ideas to the table and the value of the broad array of experiences and background that people bring to a team. It also helps group members to listen to others and work together as a team.

Description. Separate the larger group into equal small groups. Provide each small group with a note pad and a writing instrument. Let the group know that the object of this activity is for the team to create a long and creative sentence. Each team is provided a starting phrase for a sentence. Without any discussion, team members take turns adding a word onto the existing phrase. The note pad is passed on from person to person. At the end of one minute, the activity leader calls time and the last person holding the note pad finishes up the sentence using one or two words.

After you have called time, have each group count the number of words that have been added to the sentence starter. Have each group announce the number of words and read the sentence to the whole group. After each small group reads its sentence, have the other groups comment on the sentence in terms of length and creativity.

Ask the group to have dialogue about their learning in regard to the activity and how it worked for them. Be sure they explore both the positives and the challenges of the activity. Next, have them repeat the process but change the procedures. In this round, group members still must pass the paper and pencil around the group, but the group may talk about ideas for the addition of the word by each of the members. The group still will have only 60 seconds to complete the activity. After the activity, have group members share the amount of words generated and ask them to read their sentences aloud. Have them debrief this second round of the session, talking about implications and how it was different the second time around. Have them generate ideas about how this activity could be helpful to their team.

Equipment. For this activity, the groups will need several note pads and a writing instrument. You can develop your own sentence-starting prompts or consider some of the following:

- The cow jumped . . .
- A worm crawled . . .
- A loud crash . . .
- People who are . . .
- The next time . . .
- A woman screamed . . .
- One dark night . . .

Conclusion of Task. The activity is concluded when the groups have had at least two attempts at completing the sentence, one without talking and one with the ability to talk. It is important to spend the time the group needs in order to debrief the activity properly.

(Adapted from *More Activities That Teach*, by Tom Jackson, 1999)

Mental Team Building: Rising Tower

Effective problem-solving and communication strategies are essential to effective team operation. This activity provides group members an opportunity to practice and refine both of these skills.

Description. This activity can be performed as a whole team or in small subgroups of the larger team. The object is to build the highest free-standing tower possible using only toothpicks and marshmallows. Participants are given toothpicks and marshmallows and asked to work together on the project. Each team is given 15 minutes to plan and construct the tower. The tower must be able to stand freely for at least 15 seconds in order to be measured for the contest. Participants can use any construction method of their choosing. The tower will only be measured for its height from the building surface to its top.

Equipment. Each team will need a box of 500 toothpicks, a bag of mini marshmallows, and a sturdy building surface.

Conclusion of the Task. At the conclusion of the 15-minute time limit, each group must stop its progress on the tower. Each group supports its tower until the facilitator comes around to measure it. Then the tower must stand on its own for 15 seconds before it is measured. The heights of all the towers should be plotted on a chart. The group with the highest tower is declared the winner.

If you only have one team building the tower or you want to eliminate the competition between groups, challenge the group(s) to build a tower of a set length. You have to determine a good height and announce that you want the team members to work together to build a tower at or beyond that length. The height that a tower can reach varies greatly, but it is not out of the question to find towers that reach 10 to 14 inches.

Be sure to spend some time debriefing the activity. Ask the group members to reflect on what they learned about each other and their team as a result of the activity. Members normally find that they are able to identify their processing and communication strengths as a result of this activity.

Mental Team Building: Jelly Bean Questions

People can have a hard time communicating together as a team. This mental team-building activity is designed to give people a chance to learn more about each other and communicate more effectively as a group.

Description. The Jelly Bean Questions activity helps team members communicate and get to know more about each other in a structured way. It can be used for small or large groups. Each participant is given a clear plastic bag with an assortment of colored jelly beans inside. They are also given a sheet that contains questions that are color-coded to the jelly beans in the bag. One at a time, participants are asked to choose one jelly bean from their bag and answer the question that corresponds to the color of that bean. Group members go around the group or table until everyone has had a chance to answer one question. Once an initial question has been answered, the team engages in a second round. Facilitators can let team members select their own bean color or draw one each round at random. In the end, group members should engage in a brief dialogue about what they learned about each other as a result of the activity.

Equipment. To complete this activity, you will need an assortment of jelly beans that contain four to six different colors. There should be enough beans so that group members have two to three jelly beans of each color in their plastic bag. Each team member will also need a small, clear sandwich bag in which to place the beans. Finally, a list of questions corresponding to the various bean colors should be included for each team member. Such a list could include the following:

♦ Red: Name a famous person from history you would like to meet.
♦ Yellow: What is your favorite author's name and the name of his or her book?
♦ Blue: If you had one wish, what would it be?
♦ Green: Share a meaningful story or event that happened to you while you were in school.
♦ Purple: Share a meaningful story or event that happened while you were teaching children.

As you think about implementing this activity with your group, be sure to generate questions that will help the members get to know more about each other. The more they know and understand, the better they will function together as a team.

Conclusion of the Task. This activity is concluded when you feel it has served its purpose. In some groups, people have found value in completing all the questions on the sheet, while in others, just doing two or three has helped serve its purpose. The activity should be stopped if you sense a lowering of the energy level in group members.

CONFLICT RESOLUTION

In any group or community, conflict is inevitable. This can happen in interdependent groups as well as groups that are not well connected. In interdependent groups, the members see conflict as a natural part of the process of working together. These groups usually have strategies in place to deal with conflict should it arise.

Garmston and Wellman (1999) discuss two types of conflict and their impact on team operation: cognitive and affective conflict. Table 4.1 from their book defines each type of conflict and labels the impact of each on a team.

Cognitive conflict seems to be helpful to teams because it helps members to get to know more about each other. Cognitive conflict also centers around members defining important issues such as philosophy,

Table 4.1

Cognitive Conflict	Affective Conflict
Disagreements about substantive differences of opinion improve team effectiveness and produce	Disagreements over personalized, individually oriented matters reduce team effectiveness and produce
Better decisions	Destructive conflict
Increased commitment	Poorer decisions
Increased cohesiveness	Decreased commitment
Increased empathy	Decreased cohesiveness
Increased understanding	Decreased empathy

core understanding of educational principles, and other topics that the team will need to understand in order to make educational decisions.

Affective conflict, on the other hand, revolves around issues that don't impact the core working relationships of team members. The personal disagreements, personal habits, and other behaviors that can irritate team members really don't impact the core operation of a team, but these issues are important and need to be addressed before they become major issues. The norms that were introduced in Chapter 3 is one way that teams work through potentially irritating personal behaviors and habits.

Facilitators are well served to spend some time with teams to talk about the issue of conflict and how it can impact team operation. In the following examples, the facilitators deal with conflict differently, based on the conflict type and the group's need to work through the issues.

1. Matt, the facilitator of a group, has noticed that his team has been in conflict over the issue of community involvement over a decision it has been asked to make regarding the design of the new high school. Several members of the design group have said that the preliminary plans need to be open to the public, while others would like a chance to work with the architect to work out any problems in the plans before they are brought to the public for their input. Several group members have asked Matt to make the decision on the issue, but he has refused and has given it back to the group to solve. While it is taking them time to work through the decision, the two sides are beginning to see the opposite side of the issue. Eventually, they think they can work out the decision.

2. Deanne is working with a group that is trying to define the scope of a project for a new school information sign. The group members have been in conflict because of the behavior of some of its members. Several team members constantly come to meetings late, and others have been holding side conversations during the meetings. Deanne introduces ground rules to deal with the situation. As the team begins to work through its problems, she wants to gradually have the team develop a set of operating norms to help it through these personality issues.

In each of these examples, the facilitator handled the situation in a different manner. Matt let his group work through its conflict because it was cognitive in nature. The group could learn from the experience of working through the conflict. Deanne, on the other hand, needed to intervene in regard to her conflict as soon as possible. The affective conflict could have torn her team apart. For more information regarding team norms and ground rules, see Chapter 3.

Conflict is easy to see. Most facilitators can observe it from their unique perspective. There are some natural behaviors to look for when working with a group. Several are listed here:

♦ Two members are not interacting or talking together.
♦ The group seems like it wants to move on to the next issue or topic without fully discussing or solving the present issues.
♦ People are huddling and talking during breaks or interaction periods.
♦ The group is unresponsive or extremely quiet during discussions.
♦ Certain segments of the group do not want to talk or interact.
♦ Members agree on a topic without much discussion or interaction.
♦ Unusual group or individual behavior is observed that indicates conflict is present.

Most of the behaviors listed above seem to be in the area of affective conflict. When affective conflict is present on a team, the facilitator needs to take action. In addition to instituting ground rules and working to develop group norms, consider the following actions to mediate conflict.

Mediating Conflict

Facilitators of teams may face situations where people try to put them in the middle of their disagreements. Consider these strategies to put the ball back in their court and the responsibility back on those involved in the conflict:

◆ Remain as neutral as possible.
◆ Let those involved in the conflict know that your role is not to solve their problem; if possible, you would rather not get involved.
◆ If one of the parties in the conflict approaches you trying to tell his or her side of the story, direct this person back to the source of the conflict.
◆ While sending a party away to deal with the conflict, be sure to communicate your empathy regarding the situation.
◆ Avoid being put in a position to carry information from one party to another involved in the conflict.

Mediation Checklist

When you choose to help the parties involved in the conflict work through their issues, consider the following steps:

◆ Be sure that all parties in conflict are in the room.
◆ Place yourself somewhat between the conflicting parties, but sit so that you are not in the direct line of emotional fire.
◆ Open the conversation by stating your awareness of the problem or situation, and state why you are getting involved and have asked them to come together.
◆ Set the ground rules for the interaction and communication in the meeting (no name calling, listening while the other person is talking, etc.).
◆ Open the session by asking one of the parties in conflict to state his or her perspective while the other party listens. Be sure to take notes of what was presented.
◆ Allow the other person or party to share his or her side of the story in regard to the conflict.
◆ During the time the parties are describing the situation, make no comments that would make it appear that you have taken a side or formed an opinion.
◆ Summarize what you have heard so far in the discussion and ask the parties in conflict to share a perception of what has caused the conflict.
◆ Ask the parties to state what they would like to see happen in order for the conflict to be resolved.
◆ Summarize what you have heard up to this point and ask participants to agree on a plan to resolve this conflict.
◆ Help the parties in conflict to develop a follow-up plan to make sure it stays on track. Discuss possible situations where the plan could run into trouble.

◆ Summarize the growth you have seen in both parties; thank them for resolving the issues.

During your session, be careful not to get pulled into the conflict, take sides, or solve the problem for the participants. Be sure to find ways to protect yourself from the negative energy that the individuals in conflict will be emitting during this discussion.

Role of Conflict on a Team

In leading a group, leaders are taught the importance of keeping the meeting smooth and positive. In facilitating a group, facilitators should remember that it may be good for group members to experience some level of conflict. Here are some of the positive roles of conflict in a group or team:

◆ Helps a team to define its purpose
◆ Assists a group in developing team norms or behaviors
◆ Builds strength or resiliency
◆ Allows team members to get to know each other and the strengths and weaknesses of the team
◆ Lets group members experience alternative thoughts and ideas
◆ Bonds a group together, forms a sense of team

Left unchecked, however, conflict can be damaging to a team. Here are some of the ways that conflict can be damaging to team operations.

◆ Conflict sets up behavior expectations of team members (some members may feel it is their role to cause conflict, others may see themselves as mediators, etc.).
◆ People on your team may resist coming to meetings in order to avoid conflict.
◆ The focus on conflict may keep team members from accomplishing the tasks it was assigned.
◆ Certain members of the group that like conflict may gain power as a result of the constant presence of it on a team.
◆ A large amount of energy can be used by team members in dealing with conflict.

CONFLICT AND CHAOS

Conflict is closely related to another energy source found in teams called chaos. In chaos, the team members have lost some of their control over certain aspects of their operation or their scope of control in a situation. Dr. Margaret Wheatley, in her book *Leadership and the New Science* (1994), calls chaos a positive force that helps us to redefine ourselves. She also states that most groups have to experience some form of chaos in order to come out of the situation better than when they went in. Here are some forms of chaos that groups may experience:

- ◆ Unclear expectations
- ◆ Changing direction
- ◆ Reduced budgets for their decision to be implemented under
- ◆ Changing leadership
- ◆ Unclear procedures for team operation
- ◆ Disagreement among team members
- ◆ Attempt by the group to manage problems outside its control
- ◆ Disruptions with the team process caused by outside groups

Chaos is one of the stages that Peck (1987) has identified as a part of the process a group can pass through in developing community. While chaos is important to a group, there are some ideas to keep in mind in relation to chaos and the development of community:

- ◆ Understand that chaos is a natural force that most groups and organizations go through in order to form a group or community. Small doses of chaos can be good for a team, while large doses can cause trouble.
- ◆ While it might be tempting to introduce chaos to a group, be careful with this strategy; there is probably enough chaos occurring naturally to provide a team the opportunity to work through it.
- ◆ As a facilitator of groups, you will notice that as the team is experiencing chaos, members will want to quickly move out of it and may ask you to provide answers to their problems instead of working through them on their own. Don't rescue them right away.
- ◆ As your group is experiencing chaos, you may not feel that you are doing a good job in facilitating the team. Resist this and know that by letting the group work through the chaos, you are helping it work toward community.

PROTECTING TEAM MEMBERS DURING THE DECISION-MAKING PROCESS

Interdependent teams find ways to help each other during the decision-making process. When a group is formed, it is a natural occurrence for those outside the decision process to try to influence the outcome of the decision. Interdependent teams find ways to help each other as they try to deal with this outside interference. Here are some of the strategies employed by effective teams:

♦ Individual team members meet with their constituent groups and ask members not to try to influence the decision with other members of the team.

♦ Team members meet with constituents and overview the decision process, highlighting the opportunities they will have to provide input into the decision.

♦ Team members agree to support each other during the decision-making process.

♦ Individuals meet with their constituents when they hear that they have tried to influence the decision of the team.

♦ Team members agree not to discuss the proceedings of team meetings unless all team members agree to do so.

♦ The decision-making team designs informational releases so that all team members have the same information to share.

PROTECTING TEAM MEMBERS WHEN ANNOUNCING THE RESULTS OF THEIR DECISIONS

At times, teams may need to deliver unpleasant or negative messages as a result of their work on a particular issue. Interdependent groups find ways to protect each other when they have to deliver these kinds of messages. The following list contains ideas that have been used successfully when teams have had to deliver negative messages:

1. **Understand your role in the decision.** You probably did not cause the original problem. Don't feel guilty about the solution.

2. **Get your own emotions under control.** If you are feeling grounded, you will help the group stay under control as well.

3. **Know your group.** Think about the types of messages and the language that may upset them. Use methods that you know will help them to relax.

4. **Frame the message.** Use the framing tools that are highlighted in this book to help "shape" the message.

5. **Direct emotions away from you.** Use charts, handouts, multimedia, or gesturing to make the materials carry the emotion of the message.

KEEPING UNINVOLVED STAKEHOLDER
GROUPS INFORMED ABOUT THE DECISION PROGRESS

Decision-making teams face a potential problem in their operation. When the members meet to discuss the issues and information regarding a decision, they risk the chance of being seen as elite and privileged by their peers who are not involved in making the decision. This situation was identified in the book *Organizing for Successful School-Based Management* (1997) by Wohlstetter, Van Kirk, Robertson, and Mohrman. These researchers found that when a team is given a task to complete, it usually meets away from the rest of the stakeholders. If overt, purposeful, and two-way communication channels are not established early in the decision-making process, the stakeholders will soon lose respect for the team and may perceive that the team is isolated and removed from reality in relation to the decision. This is the very criticism that the team was formed to eliminate in the first place.

There are several considerations that must be taken into account when working with a team to keep this from happening:

♦ Be sure to be clear in setting up the scope of the decision so that everyone knows exactly what the team will be deciding.

♦ Establish times when information and updates will be provided to stakeholders not involved in making the primary decision but who will be directly impacted by its results.

♦ Design overt ways to gather information to be used in the decision from stakeholder groups. Some good methods include facilitated input sessions, focus groups, and surveys.

♦ Develop common information methods that can be used to make sure stakeholders get the same message at the same time. These include

– Newsletters published by the decision-making team
– Information sessions offered to all stakeholders at the same time where the information is presented by one or more team members at the same time
– Information published on a Web site and announced to all at the same time
– Official team information published on team letterhead; any other information is deemed as not "official" and incorrect
– Focus group conducted by core team members. Since each group is facilitated by the same team members, the information received is the same

In thinking about the information needs of groups, consider the planning template shown in Table 4.2.

Table 4.2   Information Planning Template

Use this template to plan the effective gathering and dissemination of information by your decision-making team. What stakeholder groups will be impacted by the decision your team is working to develop? What other groups might need to be consulted in regard to this decision?

1. What information will your group need in order to make its decision? Which groups have this information? If these groups don't have the needed information, how will you obtain it?

_____

_____

_____

2. How will you go about gathering this information in a manner that is apparent to the impacted stakeholder groups? What kinds of tools will you use to gather this information?

_____

_____

_____

3. As your team considers the decisions it is charged to make, what kinds of informational updates will the impacted stakeholders need in order to feel up to date and informed? How often will they need the information?

_____

_____

_____

4. What methods will your team use to inform stakeholders of the progress the team is making on its tasks? How will you ensure that everyone gets the same information and at the same time? What kinds of information are not ready for release at this time?

_____

_____

_____

5. How will your team evaluate its information-gathering and dissemination strategies? What changes will you make as a result of this information?

_____

_____

_____

_____

SUMMARY

In this chapter, the importance of developing an interdependent team is discussed. As a team works together, it needs to be able to form tight relationships that can help it as it encounters the possibility of conflict and chaos, two forces inevitable for teams. Conflict can be a good force for a team to work through, especially if it is of a cognitive nature. Teams also go through a variety of stages to form a true community, and facilitators can help a team by providing the freedom for the group to move through the various stages as developmentally appropriate. Finally, the need for two-way, accurate information is presented. If a group is to remain functional and credible, the information flow needs to be an overt action by the team.

In the next chapter, we explore ideas to maximize the performance and work of the teams being facilitated. This maximized performance not only helps the team function well in its capacity but makes the facilitation process a pleasure.

Reaching Peak Performance

Connecting Their Minds

Well done is better than well said.

—Ben Franklin

There is more in us than we know. If we can be made to see it, perhaps, for the rest of our lives, we will be unwilling to settle for less.

—Kurt Hahn (Outward Bound founder)

Facilitators work to maximize group energy. They do this through the way that they structure participation activities. If a group's energy is too high, the members may move too quickly on a task and not think through all the alternatives for their task. If the energy of a group is too low, its members will get bored and lose their enthusiasm for the task. In this chapter, I discuss strategies for maximizing team energy. Use the following focusing questions to track the concepts presented in this chapter:

- ♦ How can facilitators diagnose their group's level of energy?
- ♦ When would a facilitator want to lower the energy of a group?
- ♦ When would a facilitator want to raise the energy level of a group?

♦ What are some processing activities that can either raise or lower a group's energy?

♦ How can grouping team members impact their energy levels?

THE NEED TO MINIMIZE/MAXIMIZE ENERGY

One of the core functions of a facilitator is to maintain an optimal energy level for the participants on the team, committee, or task force. This management of energy serves several important functions to a team:

♦ Groups need an optimal amount of energy to stay engaged with the process.

♦ When the right amount of energy is present in group members, their thinking and problem-solving skills are at their best.

♦ The right amount of energy helps group members develop a collaborative relationship.

♦ If the energy level of a group gets too low, the group gets sluggish; if the energy level is to high, the group can get confrontational.

DIAGNOSING GROUP ENERGY

Facilitators observe their groups to decide if the energy level is too high or too low. The following questions provide a guide for this observational process:

♦ Is the group moving too quickly and not thinking though all the possible implications of its work? (If yes, too high)

♦ Are one or two members the only people contributing? (If yes, too low)

♦ Have members appeared to check out of the discussion? (If yes, too low)

♦ Does it seem that tempers are flaring a little? (If yes, too high)

♦ Is the group's patience wearing thin? (If yes, too high)

♦ Does the group seem nervous or upset? (If yes, too high)

♦ Are you getting low-level answers or ideas? (If yes, too low)

♦ Are you providing most of the suggestions and ideas? (If yes, too low)

WORKING/PROCESSING COMBINATIONS

The way in which facilitators ask groups or teams to process or work with information can either raise or lower the energy level. The following list contains a sample of some of the processing activities and their normal impact on group energy. These ideas can be quickly implemented without much background preparation.

◆ Talk in pairs or groups smaller than four: increases energy
◆ Individually write a response to a question: decreases energy
◆ Share responses one at a time with the entire group: decreases energy
◆ Members stand and interact with other team members: increases energy
◆ Group members listen to information presented to them by facilitator or outside presenter: decreases energy
◆ Small groups meet and put responses on chart paper: increases energy

In thinking about the examples given here, it is important to remember that one group may react differently to a processing strategy than another group. Be sure to take a group's unique characteristics into account when implementing a processing strategy.

GROUPING AND REGROUPING STRATEGIES

In order for groups to be productive, the members have to be able to see the issues they face from a variety of perspectives. People in groups want to stay in their comfort zone as they begin to generate solutions to the problems their organizations face. One way to help people open up their thinking is to have them mix with others on the team. When they regroup, they are able to work with others and gain important perspectives other than those they may share with the people they always work with on a team. Here are a set of nonconfrontational grouping strategies that can impact the energy level of a group.

Playing Cards

In order to establish a random grouping, facilitators can use a standard deck of playing cards. As people enter the room, they are given a card and told they will use it later. At the time in the meeting when people need to be rearranged into groups, the facilitator can ask members to regroup by finding their corresponding card matches. This strategy works well and helps people regroup with minimal confrontation. Here are the major steps in the process:

1. Give each person a standard playing card. Make sure you have counted the people in the room and set up the playing card groups to fit your needs. For example, if you want groups of four, then

you need to have people regroup by card value such as king, ace, and so on. If you need a group of six, you need to place six cards of each suit in the deck you use and ask people to look for corresponding suits to form their groups.

2. When you need people to change groups, announce that they need to regroup, but use their playing cards to form a new group. Go over the procedure and have them move.

3. Once they regroup, have them turn in their cards and get them started on the next activity.

Variations: For variety, consider using cards other than playing cards such as baseball cards, children's game cards, Monopoly cards, or any other cards that allow you to group people in a random fashion.

Number Groups

Another way to assign random groups is to use numbers. There are a variety of ways to assign numbers and then regroup based on those numbers. Here are a few:

♦ Write the numbers on name tags.
♦ Write numbers on handouts.
♦ Have participants number off by threes, fours, fives, or whatever combination is needed to form a team.
♦ Have number disks; ask participants to select a disk from a basket and find their matching numbers.
♦ Write numbers on the bottom of plates, cups, or on napkins.
♦ Write numbers on small, flat sticks; have participants select a stick.

Whatever method you choose, be sure that the numbers are random in nature. This will ensure that you are able to regroup people in teams that will allow them to interact with people they normally don't get a chance to work with on a daily basis. It not only gives them a different perspective, but it will let them get to know people in a deeper way.

Learning Partners

This is a method that requires some planning at the beginning of a session, but one that can be pretty effective in getting people divided up in a fun and random manner. Consider the following methods for dividing up groups:

♦ Ask people to find partners based on their clothing. For example, have them find someone who has a similar shoe on, a similar blouse or shirt on, or other matching clothing items. When they connect in pairs, they should write down the name of their partner. Later in the session, when they need a random partner, you could say, "Find your shoe partner." They can go and meet that person.

♦ Direct group members to find partners based on the geographic region of their college. Keep this simple. Ask them to form partners with those from the same region their college is located in. Be sure they write down the name of their partner so they can find them later when assigned.

♦ Ask team members to group themselves by geographic location of their last vacation. Follow the same process as the college partner process listed above.

♦ Have people form groups based on their favorite season. You could have them group by favorite season, identify a partner, and then group by their second favorite season and identify a learning partner from this group.

♦ Use your imagination to generate other topics by which to base groupings on such things as favorite meal, time of day, sports activities, and other topics that may be of interest to your group.

(Adapted from *The Adaptive School: Developing and Facilitating Collaborative Groups*, by Bob Garmston and Bruce Wellman, 1997)

Generational/Diversity Groups

One of the reasons people are put into teams is to expand their background and experiences and make better decisions. The use of generational or mixed diversity groups can help in considering decisions from a variety of points of view. Here are some simple ways to set up these kinds of groups:

♦ Ask your team to stand.

♦ Have your team members form themselves into teams of four; the teams have to contain as much diversity as possible (you might consider giving them some examples of group diversity such as grade level assignments, number of years in education, gender, subject area).

♦ Let the team members know that once they have organized themselves into a foursome, they need to engage in a dialogue about how their team illustrates diversity.

♦ Once the team members have formed and discussed their diversity, they should share this with the entire group.
♦ Remind group members why they were asked to form diverse teams. Let them know how this is an advantage to their thinking and problem-solving processes.
♦ Engage the teams in discussions about the decisions and the content of the meeting.

Problem Interest Task Forces

People can be randomized by asking them to form task forces based on their topic interest. The groups should be organized into these task forces for relatively short periods of time.

In order to do this activity, keep these ideas in mind:

♦ Write the major tasks or jobs on chart paper posted around the room.
♦ Discuss each of the jobs or tasks and what needs to be done in detail; allow the group to ask questions about each of the tasks.
♦ Have group members think about which jobs or tasks are most appealing to them. Have them generate their first and second preferences for which jobs they would like to work on.
♦ Ask members to stand and walk over to the chart that has the job that they are most interested in working on; wait for everyone to get settled in at a chart.
♦ If some jobs or tasks are underrepresented or have no members interested in working within that area, ask the group to decide if those jobs are really important, if they should be put on hold, or if members from one of the other groups would be interested in working on them.
♦ Once the team members have made their final decisions, discuss the parameters for each task force in relation to timeline, duties, and other logistical items, and get the task forces started with their assignments.

OTHER GROUP PROCESSING STRATEGIES

Category Lineup

Another interesting way to divide people into small, somewhat random teams is to use a lineup. The procedures for a birthday lineup is described next. Other ideas that can follow the same format are discussed following Birthday Lineup.

Birthday Lineup

In this activity, people are asked to line up in birth and month order, and then individual members are selected to form random groups.

♦ Instruct group members that they need to form a single file in order based on their birth month and day. The line should start in one part of the room with January 1 and end in another part of the room with December 31.

♦ The group members can use any form of communication except speaking to figure out the birth month and date of their colleagues. They need to use this information to line up in the exact order of their births.

♦ Twins (people have the same month and day of birth) need to stand next to each other in the birthday line.

♦ Once the group is finished, the facilitator needs to start at the beginning of the line and ask each member to share his or her birth month and day. If there are mistakes, the group needs to correct them.

♦ The facilitator or group leader then goes down the line counting off by fours, fives, sixes, or whatever number of groups are needed. The ones all meet together, the twos next, and so on.

Variations

♦ Elaborate shoe lineup: Members line up from least to most elaborate shoe.

♦ Years of experience: People line up in order based on their years in the district.

♦ Distance from their high school: Team members line up in order from who attended the high school closest to farthest from the meeting.

♦ Small to large breakfast: People normally eating the smallest breakfast line up in the front, those eating the largest breakfast line up in the back.

♦ Other criteria: Look for other criteria for lining up that would be fun and interesting for the group to do. Think about how the group members might communicate the criteria for the lineup as one factor in helping you make a decision.

Random Name Sticks

This activity can be a good way to get people divided up into groups on a random basis. It can be used in a variety of other ways as well.

♦ Find enough small flat sticks so that there is one for every member of your group. The kinds of sticks that ice cream treats come on can be good for this activity.

♦ Write a different group member's name on each stick. Be sure to double-check to make sure that you have accounted for everyone.

♦ When you are ready to subdivide the group into smaller, more random teams, draw the group names by using the sticks.

♦ After all the team members have been placed, get the groups started on their task.

Alternative Uses of Random Name Sticks

♦ Draw name sticks for roles on the team such as secretary, convener, or whatever roles you need covered on a periodic basis.

♦ Draw name sticks for the order in which people will be asked to participate in sharing ideas with the entire team.

♦ Use name sticks as an informal way to take meeting attendance.

Dice Partners

This is another interesting way to divide people up into smaller, more random groups. It works to keep the facilitator from having to make the decision regarding separating members from each other.

♦ Depending on the group size, use two to four dice for each member.

♦ Each group member rolls the appropriate number of dice.

♦ Members are grouped together based on the numbers they roll. For large groups, it may work to put all those with corresponding numbers in the same group; for smaller groups, you may want to put all evens together, or put people who rolled less than 12 in a group, those who rolled between 12 and 24 in a group, and so on.

♦ Make sure to clearly explain the selection process so that members can quickly move through it to form their groups. These groups should be together on a short-term rather than long-term basis.

♦ As a group gets good at dividing itself into small teams, consider other options such as allowing members who rolled pairs to be together and other fun ideas to keep the group moving.

The Information Frenzy

This strategy can be used at various times in a meeting or as a way of helping people review information from previous sessions. It is quick and efficient and provides variety in processing for group members. It works like this:

- ♦ Members are asked to form teams of two.
- ♦ In each pair, one person is designated as Person A, the other is designated as Person B.
- ♦ The facilitator asks the team members to be ready to talk about the content previously presented to the group or discussed by the group. The team members must try to recall the main points of the previous discussion from what they remember; no notes may be used for review; examples are listed below in the next bulleted list.
- ♦ Person A is asked to talk about the topic from memory for 45 seconds. Person B listens to the comments made by Person A.
- ♦ At the end of the 45 seconds, the facilitator stops the discussion.
- ♦ Person B is asked to go next and talk about the topic for 45 seconds without repeating anything said by Person A.
- ♦ The discussion is stopped; Person A is asked to talk about the topic for 30 seconds without repeating anything said in the previous round; Person B listens.
- ♦ The process repeats itself through the 30-second round; if needed, the facilitator can engage the group in a third round where each party talks for 15 seconds. The facilitator needs to take the depth of topic and the attitudes of the participants into account when deciding whether or not to do a third round.

This activity may sound like it would be extremely hard for your participants, but once the initial round has been completed, they are able to think and quickly generate new ideas in the following rounds. The whole activity takes less than 5 to 6 minutes to complete but is extremely energizing for a group. Here are some possible prompts to use in starting the paired discussions:

- ♦ What have been the major topics of discussion we have had in relation to our tasks? How did these topics impact our team and its operation?
- ♦ Talk about what we have learned so far as we have examined this topic.
- ♦ What issues have we uncovered in our work together?
- ♦ Think about our progress so far. What have been the major high points of our learning so far?
- ♦ What kinds of issues do we still need to tackle as we move forward with this project?

In some situations, facilitators have asked participants to write down the major points of their discussions; others have had a third party note taker work with each pair to write down the ideas that were discussed during the Information Frenzy exercise.

(Adapted from *How to Make Presentations that Teach and Transform* by Garmston and Wellman)

Multiple Hats

This exercise energizes a group but also helps members see a topic from multiple perspectives. As the group is holding a dialogue, members are assigned a viewpoint perspective and must take this perspective as the dialogue progresses. The activity is called Multiple Hats because participants are asked to take on a different perspective or role than they normally represent or are involved with in their assignment. The perspective or "hats" that the team members take on are based on the major stakeholder groups that will be impacted by the decision. Here is how the activity works:

♦ The facilitator working with the group describes the activity, explains the importance of looking at an issue from multiple perspectives, and describes the perspectives or hats the group will be using to view a situation.
♦ Group members are assigned a perspective or hat that they need to use to shape their thoughts during the dialogue on an issue.
♦ The facilitator starts the group on its dialogue, allowing 15 to 20 minutes on the main topic.
♦ Once the dialogue is over, the facilitator asks the group members to talk about what they learned in the activity and how it will help them as they work together in the future.

As the team works through this activity, its members will become energized and engaged. It is especially meaningful if the hats chosen are pertinent to the group. Some perspectives that have worked well with groups in the past include the following:

♦ Parent
♦ Always positive
♦ Board of education
♦ Big picture view
♦ Detail view
♦ Teacher
♦ Future student (1 year after idea is implemented)
♦ Always negative
♦ Devil's advocate
♦ Community
♦ Questioning
♦ Concerned about politics of district
♦ Concerned about feelings of people
♦ Budget focused

♦ Linked to and fond of the past
♦ Keeps everyone focused on their role or hat

In some groups, the facilitator has members actually wear hats to help designate the perspective that each represents. This seems to energize groups even more than just the activity itself. At the end of the dialog, be sure to ask members to take a few minutes to talk about their learning as a result of the exercise. This helps keep the group members thinking about the importance of examining other perspectives as they tackle issues in their decision making.

(Adapted from the work of Edward DeBono)

Synectics

Synectic activities ask the group or person to draw comparisons between items, ideas, and concepts that are not naturally related. In this process, the group is engaged in the following processes:

♦ Examining each item, idea, or concept and identifying the particular core attribute of each.
♦ Comparing each unique list and searching for common points or shared attributes. If none are common, the team must draw some connection between those things being compared.
♦ Putting together a new idea or category that links the common attributes.

The process of synectics enables team members to begin the kinds of processing and thinking that will be required of them as they work toward resolving the task or problem that has been presented to them for their solution. In general, it works like this:

♦ The facilitator shows an object, cartoon, or picture.
♦ The facilitator asks group members to look at the object and think about how this object is like something the group might be dealing with at the present time (e.g., their main task, teaching in the spring, working with difficult situations).
♦ Group members are asked to share their ideas in small teams or pairs.
♦ After they have had 1 to 2 minutes to talk about their ideas, the facilitator asks group members to share their discussions with the entire team.
♦ The facilitator asks team members to discuss what they learned about their colleagues as a result of the exercise.

Examples

1. At a transitional period right after a group has taken a break in its discussion, the facilitator shows the group a one-frame cartoon. The facilitator lets the group read the cartoon and think about it and the message it is delivering for a minute, then asks group members to talk in teams of two about how this cartoon is like the academic standards the group is working to implement. After a couple of minutes, group members begin to share some funny and interesting comparisons with each other.

2. In a staff meeting, the leader of the group starts the meeting by showing the group a picture of a child riding a bicycle down a set of stairs. She asks the group members to form small groups of three or four and talk about how the picture is similar to the parent-teacher conferencing plan the group has been discussing. Several teams generate good ideas in relation to the prompt.

3. At a meeting of custodial staff, the leader tells a story about a person who worked on a shift stoking the boiler. He talks about the hard work involved in the task and the appreciation that the crew shows for the work this person has been doing to keep the ship on its course. The leader asks the group members to talk about how this story relates to the staff recognition program they are planning.

In all these examples, the person running the meeting is using the strategy of synectics to help the group think a little differently than it would have without the prompt. Consider using synectics to help engage your group in an energizing discussion.

(The term "synectics" is taken from *Pathways to Understanding*, by Laura Lipton and Bruce Wellman, 1998, and adapted for the illustrated use in this example.)

Compare/Contrast Matrix

The use of a compare/contrast matrix is a visual facilitation technique that helps to energize a group and assist its processing. Here it is used in helping a group examine the similarities or differences between ideas, concepts, or decisions, but it can be used for a variety of other purposes with a group. Here is how it works:

♦ The facilitator posts a grid or matrix, filling in the axis with the information to be discussed (see example below).

♦ The group can either talk about the issues or break into small teams to talk about the components on the grid.
♦ The group sums up its learning.

Topic	Block Scheduling	6-Period Day	7-Period Day
Similarities			
Differences			

In this example, the team would list the similarities and differences of each major scheduling type under the scheduling category listed on the chart. This exercise is helpful because it allows the team members to generate ideas in an objective fashion and it helps them to develop a visual representation of the information they may be examining more closely in the future. In the next example, a different way to use a matrix is illustrated.

Topic	Block Scheduling	6-Period Day	7-Period Day
Match with existing school practices			
New learning or structures that would be required to make the idea successful			

In the second example, the major topics remain the same as in the first example, but we have changed the processing that is now required of the participants. Here they are being asked to look at the topics from an ease of implementation perspective. After a team has completed this matrix, they would clearly understand the issues that might be associated with implementing a new idea.

While these ideas may look very simple, they can be powerful in helping a group to objectively examine several issues and to truly understand the scope of the issues. Some facilitators hold an open dialogue where people work together as one group on the matrix. Others might divide the larger team into small groups, each working on one topic within the matrix, while other groups are asked to complete the entire matrix without facilitator guidance. However it is completed, it is important to have the group talk about the completed matrix and make any changes that the entire group feels need to be made so that it reflects current thought. It is also a good idea for the group members to talk about what they have learned as a result of the activity once it is completed.

(Adapted from *Classroom Instruction That Works*, by Marzano, Pickering, and Pollock, 2001)

Three-Step Interviews

This is a strategy that has been used by colleagues Bruce Wellman and Laura Lipton in working with groups in teaching and staff development contexts. I have adapted it to help teams in decision-making and meeting situations. It allows a group to more deeply understand an issue and slows the group down so that it is able to more effectively problem-solve as a group.

Steps in a Three-Step Interview

1. Team members work in pairs; one is the interviewer, the other is the interviewee. The interviewer listens actively to the comments and thoughts of the interviewee, paraphrasing key points and significant details. Group members reverse roles, repeating the process.

2. Each pair joins another pair to form groups of four. Team members introduce their pair partner and briefly present what their partner had to say about the topic at hand. After both pairs have shared, the group draws consensus on the major points of agreement and works through issues related to points of disagreement.

3. All the groups merge and talk about consensus and disagreement points as a large team.

The three-step interview process allows a team to break a complex topic into parts and work through any potential conflict areas in a small group setting before they are brought to the larger group. Sometimes these issues work themselves out before the large group has to deal with them. Here's an example of this strategy in action.

In a recent meeting to determine the finalists for a science text adoption, Jennifer knew that at least two different camps were forming around two text series. She decided to have the team use the three-step interview process as a way of helping team members hear and understand each of the major positions before the topic moved to the larger group. She divided team members into small, random groups using playing cards (the members had to find the matching card to the one they were holding). In the three-step interview process, each team had to address the strengths and limitations of each text series. Once these were addressed, they formed teams of fours and repeated the process. As the team members were talking, Jennifer walked around the room and listened to the dialogue around the issues. She was able to hear that some of the groups were addressing their concerns in the small teams and were beginning to understand each other's perspectives. She asked each team of four to put its list of pros and cons on chart paper. At the end of the three-step process, each team presented its ideas. Most of the presentations had similar themes. Now when she held the large group discussion on the issue, the group was able to use clear information to talk about its options rather than focusing on feelings and emotions.

In this example, the three-step interview process helped to establish a base for the group to use in processing the total information. Once this base had been established, the group could go back to other existing structures to work through the issues associated with the curriculum choices.

(Adapted from *Pathways to Understanding,* by Laura Lipton and Bruce Wellman, 1998)

Fishbowls

As team members work together, they can develop certain "habitual" behaviors. The groups can fall into processing and discussion habits that allow members to have diminished energy or even impede their decision-making abilities. A fishbowl activity can be a good way to energize a group or to lower its anxiety/energy level. The name comes from the fact that the members are operating in an environment where they are visible to others, just like fish are in a clear glass bowl. Fishbowls work like this:

- ◆ Briefly describe the activity. Ask for five or six volunteers to be in the fishbowl.
- ◆ Have the volunteers sit in a circle in the middle of the room. Have everyone else sit in an outer circle.
- ◆ Give the volunteers specific instructions for a topic you'd like them to talk about. Be specific on the topic and the process you'd like them to be engaged in during the discussion. Set a time limit for the activity. Give those in the outer circle specific instructions about their role in the process and what kinds of group behaviors they are observing. Make sure that they remain quiet during the fishbowl discussion.
- ◆ When the discussion time is up, break both the inner circle and outer circle groups into small teams and have the members engage in a dialogue about their feelings and observations regarding the fishbowl discussion.

♦ Bring the large group back together. Have both those in the fishbowl and those in the outer circle talk about their feelings, understandings, and perceptions of the process. Be sure to find out what each learned in the process.

Fishbowls can be controversial in nature; be sure to think through the possible behaviors your group may exhibit as a result of a fishbowl. Some facilitators introduce the fishbowl concept to a group before the group engages in an emotion-filled or controversial topic. This helps the group learn how to work with this strategy to improve its operation.

Variations

Fishbowls allow some variations in their basic structure that can help a group get more learning from the experience. Consider the following ideas:

♦ At certain times in the fishbowl, stop the dialogue and ask for group member feelings and perceptions about the discussion process that is occurring.
♦ After a set amount of time, allow people sitting outside the fishbowl to tap in and replace members on the inner circle when they have something to contribute to the dialogue. In using this strategy, establish clear parameters for them to enter the group.
♦ Post a large chart outside the fishbowl and allow members in the outer circle to write thoughts, comments, and questions on the chart that they would like the fishbowl participants to consider in their dialogue. These comments could be viewed as "silent instructions" to those in the fishbowl.
♦ Allow fishbowl participants to substitute a member from the outer circle when they feel a need to be less visible or have a lack of information about the issue at hand.
♦ Allow fishbowl participants to call on a resource person from the outer circle to help them clarify information as needed.

(Adapted from *Facilitator's Guide to Participatory Decision-Making*, by Sam Kaner, 1996)

Forced Choice Strategies

Open discussion and dialogue can help a group work through issues, but in many cases, the emotions and feelings of members can get in the way of the group coming together on an idea or moving the decision-making process forward. Using strategies that help a group visually make choices can be very helpful in managing their energy and helping them move an issue forward. Here are some possible ideas to consider that force a choice by the group.

- ♦ **Straw voting.** Each group member is given a number of straws. The number of straws is usually less than the number of choices. Each choice is listed on a chart and has a straw container in front of the choice. Members are given a chance to walk around and place straws in their choices on an issue. The facilitator counts the straws in the containers to determine the top choices.
- ♦ **Colored sticky notes.** Team members are given sticky note pads with a color-coding scheme. For example, red means first choice, blue means second choice, and so on. Group members place their sticky pad sheets by the topic of their first, second, third, and so on choices. Points are assigned for the choice positions and the totals are added up at the end. The choices are prioritized by the number of points received.
- ♦ **Conflict coding.** Group members are asked to examine a list of possible solutions and mark the choices where a conflict occurs for them. At the end, the choices with the least marks are moved forward for further consideration. I used this recently to help a group set up a series of meeting dates for future discussions. All the possible dates for meetings were listed on a calendar. Group members were given a set amount of time outside the normal meeting structure to mark those dates that contained unchangeable conflicts. The conflict markings were analyzed by a small team from the larger group, and decisions were made based on the data from the group about the future meeting dates.
- ♦ **"Stand by my decision."** This strategy involves having the group do what the name implies. Each member gets a set number of votes. When the facilitator calls out the category, group members stand by their choices. Since each group member is allowed only a certain number of choices, the facilitator is able to gauge the interest and support for each of the strategies.
- ♦ **"Take off the table."** In this activity, each of the ideas or suggestions starts off with a set number of sticky pad sheets posted on a chart containing a table graphic listing the idea. Members are allowed to take off a set number of sticky pad sheets from the tables. In the end, those tables that have the most sticky pad sheets remaining on them are the highest priorities for the group to consider.

All of these forced choice strategies help a group to lower the emotions associated with a topic and calmly work through the decision-making process. Consider how your group typically handles itself during processing in order to make a decision about whether or not to use forced choice decision-making tools.

Gallery Walks

An interesting and informative way to help a team look at issues and keep its energy at an optimal level is to employ the strategy of a gallery walk. In a gallery walk, team members are asked to examine issues and develop their own conclusions about the issues based on their observations. In general, a Gallery Walk works like this:

- ◆ Members of the group are divided into subgroups or task forces.
- ◆ Each task force is given the assignment to examine an issue from a unique perspective or to look at a specific aspect of an issue.
- ◆ The subgroup places its work on chart paper using unique ways to show its work such as drawing pictures, using charts, or developing other meaningful products.
- ◆ Once these have been completed, their "products" are posted in an area of the room that is separate from the main meeting area. Each task force or work group has its own unique area for display.
- ◆ All the members are instructed to walk through the gallery as a team to learn what the other teams have done. Their team members need to make any notes they feel would be helpful in holding a discussion after the Gallery Walk.
- ◆ After the walk, each team is given some time to engage in a dialogue around the ideas the members observed and the issues that were raised during the walk.
- ◆ After the individual dialogues are completed, the entire team or group talks about the learning that occurred in the process.

Gallery Walks can be used for a variety of other group processing opportunities. Be sure to use the gallery terminology. It helps to set an emotional tone and keeps the dialogue on a positive note in the process. Some positive transfer occurs around the concept of the gallery that you want to use in managing the energy of the team or group. Most people have been to a gallery of some kind in their lives and know that a gallery is a place for thinking and reflection. They transfer these ideas to the process they engage in with their teams.

Example

In looking at helping a school staff close down its implementation of a data-driven school improvement project, William asked departments to meet for 15 minutes and put together a meaningful

Table 5.1   Planning Template

Processing and Thinking

Use this template as you begin to think about your planning in relation to helping people to think and process during a facilitation session:

1. How much thinking and processing will be required for your group to work through the task it has been assigned?

_____

_____

_____

2. How has your group done in this area in the past?

_____

_____

_____

3. What kinds of regrouping and processing activities seem to fit the culture of your team?

_____

_____

_____

4. List the strategies you are planning to implement and where they will be integrated into the agenda.

_____

_____

_____

5. How will you give the group the rationale for why they need to work with others in completing their task?

_____

_____

_____

6. How will you assess the effectiveness of the processing and regrouping strategies that you have chosen to implement with this group?

_____

_____

_____

7. What kinds of materials and supplies will you need to be successful?

_____

_____

_____

graphic that would sum up their greatest accomplishments within the project on half a sheet of chart paper. On the other half of the paper, they were asked to illustrate their greatest challenge with the project for the future. After the work time had expired, William asked each department to display their chart with the other charts around the room. He then had group members walk through the gallery of displays and talk about what kinds of trends members saw in the various chart presentations. In the end, the entire group used this experience to sum up the learning that had occurred in the project and to set goals for their second year of implementation.

Planning Template

Use the planning template in Table 5.1 to plan your use of regrouping strategies to help your group members reach peak performance. By thinking about this aspect of team operation and planning your activities in advance, you will increase the chance of providing your team a good processing experience.

SUMMARY

One role of the facilitator is to keep the energy level of each group that is going through the process at an optimal level to help the group stay on track and focused during its time together. The strategies presented in this chapter provide the facilitator with an opportunity to diagnose the level of energy present in the group, then put a strategy in place to increase or decrease the energy level while engaging the team members in processing content related to their task. It is important for the facilitator to think through the use of these strategies in advance, since each group's reaction to them may be slightly different. This will ensure a positive experience for both the facilitator and the team members.

Working the Brain

6

The true test of a first-rate mind is the ability to hold two contradictory ideas at the same time.

—F. Scott Fitzgerald

A closed mind is a dying mind.

—Edna Ferber

As facilitators work with groups, they find that empowering the group to generate lots of ideas to consider for the final solution makes the team productive. One way that teams generate lots of ideas is with the use of a technique called brainstorming.

Use the following focusing questions to guide your thoughts as you read this chapter:

- ♦ Why do we want to use brainstorming to get ideas generated?
- ♦ What are the important attributes to consider in brainstorming?
- ♦ What are some techniques that can help groups do an effective job in brainstorming?

BRAINSTORMING TECHNIQUES

In general, asking a group to participate in a brainstorm on a particular topic increases its energy level. The very term *brainstorming* denotes an accelerated pattern of thinking. In order to build the high energy level needed for brainstorming, the group has to have some rules. Consider the following:

◆ There needs to be a defined, constrained time for the activity.
◆ The goal of the group is to get lots of ideas on the table for consideration.
◆ No comments pro or con may be made in response to any idea shared until all considerations are exhausted.
◆ Once all the ideas are listed, the group members can then begin the process of deepening their understanding of each and evaluating them to see if they have merit for possibilities for the team to consider.

Many classroom teachers use brainstorming with their children on a regular basis, but they don't consider using the skill when working with adult groups. Brainstorming can be a productive way to help a group generate a wide variety of possibilities for the solutions to problems the group is facing or to generate ideas for improvement. Keep the following in mind when brainstorming with adult groups:

◆ Adults may be inhibited in participating in brainstorming when it is first introduced. It can be hard for people to shout out an answer because they may worry about being wrong. Lower the level of concern in the initial stages by asking people to list their ideas on paper or talk about possibilities in small groups before you ask them to share their thoughts with the larger group.
◆ Explain the process to the team up front and let them know that the ideas may come slowly when they first engage in the process. This lets them know that it's OK if they have a hard time with the skill in the opening stages.
◆ Explain to the members that you will be using "wait time" to let them think and come up with their ideas. Give yourself permission to allow silence as you are waiting for the group to answer.
◆ Be careful in reinforcing the answers given to you by individuals on the team. You may actually make people more resistant to sharing, since they may think that the answers you praise or reinforce are really good. They may not think that their answer will merit a "good job" from you.
◆ Lighten up the group by telling the members that they can feed you ideas as fast as you can write them down. During the initial stages of the process, their ideas will get ahead of you and the group will enjoy watching you try to catch up. After an idea is written on the chart, put a slash or dot below it to signify that you are expecting one more idea. This will prime the pump and help people keep generating ideas to fill in your slash marks.

♦ When it seems like the members have generated all the possible responses, wait, then engage them to think about more ideas. This could be accomplished by

- Telling group members that they have to come up with three more ideas before moving off the present topic
- Asking members to meet in pairs or triplets to generate more ideas
- Temporarily stopping the brainstorm and asking team members to write more ideas on paper; once ideas have been generated, move back to the group brainstorming process
- Using one of the alternative brainstorming strategies listed later in this chapter to change the process and energize the team members

♦ Avoid asking a group member to write the responses generated in the brainstorm. The team may need all the minds they can get to participate in the brainstorming process in order to generate a wide variety of responses. The facilitator should take the notes from the brainstorming session. This allows the facilitator to pace the brainstorming session and manage the energy of the team generating the ideas.
♦ Hold true to the steps of brainstorming and thank the team members for their total contributions.

BRAINSTORMING STRATEGIES AND IDEAS

The remainder of this chapter contains brainstorming ideas that can be used as a first attempt to get lots of ideas out on the table or as extensions of other brainstorming techniques when a group has exhausted all the obvious ideas.

Add 5

In this strategy, the person facilitating the discussion encourages the group members to deepen their idea generation session by having them add five new ideas onto the list they have already generated. When members have brainstormed a list of ideas, they sometimes stop after the obvious or easy ideas are listed. A helpful prompt by the facilitator can get the group to generate a more extended list of ideas. Here are the steps typically involved:

- ◆ The group brainstorms ideas and appears to run out of new ideas for the list.
- ◆ The facilitator says to the group, "We will be finished when we get five more ideas on the chart."
- ◆ The facilitator makes five slash marks or bullet points on the chart.
- ◆ The facilitator encourages people to add more until the goal is reached and pauses to wait for the ideas to be generated.
- ◆ The facilitator can set the number of new ideas for the group to brainstorm.

While this strategy may seem simple to implement, it is important for the facilitator to pause and allow the group to brainstorm the desired list of new ideas.

Example

"Today, you have generated an extensive list of ideas for our group to consider in addressing our decision. Sometimes, groups seem to run out of ideas and stop brainstorming too early, since some really good solutions may not have yet been identified. Let's take 10 more minutes and identify five more ideas on our chart. [Facilitator draws five slash marks on chart paper, then steps back to give the group thinking time]. All right, let's go. Just share your ideas and I'll jot then down. [First idea] Thanks, we have four more to go." Facilitator encourages and reinforces ideas as they are generated until the group reaches the desired number.

Modality/Learning Style

In this strategy, the facilitator provides the group an assist to help it generate more ideas. It can be used as a brainstorming idea itself or can be added to another strategy. The group is asked to generate ideas that are focused on certain learning or processing styles. This activity follows this procedure:

- ◆ The group is asked to generate ideas that specifically relate to a certain learning modality of style such as visual, auditory, or kinesthetic.
- ◆ The facilitator either provides a location for these ideas on the existing chart or provides a new chart for the generation of the ideas related to the specific learning modality being generated.
- ◆ Once the group has slowed down its generation of ideas, the facilitator stops the brainstorm, gives the group another learning modality to generate ideas around, and starts the process over again.

♦ Normally, this process shifts between two or three modalities before the facilitator calls an end to the brainstorm.

♦ Once the ideas are generated, the group begins to question and evaluate the appropriateness of the ideas.

Example

"As we work together today, we are going to generate a list of possible ideas that our site council needs to consider in setting up our career day. [Group brainstorms a list of 15 or 20 ideas.] In order to help us think of more possibilities, we need to spend the next 5 minutes thinking about ideas that involve seeing or vision. [Group adds six or seven new thoughts to the list.] We've added more good possibilities to this list. Let's try looking at ideas related to listening or sound. [Group lists seven or eight more.] Great. Now that we have an expanded list, let's clarify these and begin to evaluate some of the possible choices we now have for our career day."

In this example, you notice that the person facilitating the group decided to just try two learning modality brainstorms. She made this decision because she sensed that the group was getting tired and had worked on this part of the decision-making process long enough for the present time.

Color/Characteristic

This technique can be used as either an initial or expansion activity to add to a list that was brainstormed using another technique. The person facilitating can use the following steps:

♦ The facilitator looks at the list that has been generated by the group and thinks about characteristics/colors that may help the group expand the list.

♦ The group is directed to brainstorm ideas related to the identified color/characteristic.

Jeremy, a teacher facilitating a school-based team that has been charged with the task of designing the criteria that will be used to evaluate materials for a math adoption, used characteristic brainstorming to expand an initial list of ideas generated by the team:

"Our group has brainstormed a fairly extensive list of criteria we need to keep in mind in evaluating materials for our math text adoption. Before we make a decision on the final evaluation criteria, we need to add a few more ideas to the list for us to consider. For the next 5 minutes, I want you to think of ideas that involve the characteristic of student interest in the materials. [Group lists several criteria that the committee could use to evaluate the materials on student interest.] Now let's look at generating a list of possible criteria that could be used to judge problem-solving opportunities. [The group generates several criteria that could help determine the amount and quality of the problem-solving opportunities in the potential math materials. Once the new criteria have been added to the list, Jeremy asks the team members engaged in the brainstorm to clarify and prioritize their top five evaluation criteria and begin to form a plan to examine math materials.]"

After the team members eliminated 8 of the original criteria from the list and focused on 10 observable and measurable criteria, they were able to put together a sound and comprehensive plan to select the proper math materials for their school district.

Alternate Chart

This brainstorming activity takes advantage of the nature of groups to be focused and active at the beginning of the process, but to lose some of their energy after a few minutes into the process. It can be implemented with any number of charts but seems to work best when the group is limited to two or three rotations. It works like this:

◆ The group is divided up into small teams of three or four people.
◆ The categories that need to be brainstormed are arranged around the room. Usually the number of charts varies from two to three. It is important to have enough charts to allow free rotation but not so many charts that the teams are overwhelmed with the activity.
◆ Have each of the small teams stand by one of the posted charts to start the activity. Let each team brainstorm and write down as many ideas as it can for a short period of time (usually 3 to 4 minutes).
◆ At the end of the brainstorming time, call "Switch." This is a signal to the teams that they need to move to another chart. If there are four charts in the room, have them go to the one that is opposite where they are standing. If there is an odd number of charts, send them to a random location; try to avoid just having them rotate clockwise to another chart.
◆ Have the teams visit each chart two or three times, then stop the activity; have the entire group go through the process of getting

clarity on the ideas before the group makes any decisions on the ideas brainstormed.

Example

"During the next few minutes, we will be brainstorming ideas for how to form partnerships between the school and community. In the room you can see that there are four charts posted. The categories listed on these charts are (1) ways the school can benefit the community, (2) ways the community can help the schools, (3) existing initiatives that can provide a base for future projects, and (4) people who need to be on the design committee for this project."

"At your seating location is a card with a number on it. Find the other members of your group who have a matching number. [Group does and clusters together in small teams of two or three.] Grab a marker and stand by one of the charts posted in the room. When I say 'Go,' write down as many ideas as your team can think of on the chart in front of you. [Teams do.] Stop. Now turn around and look at the chart behind you. [Teams do.] Go to that chart and write as many ideas as you can think of in 3 minutes. [Facilitator keeps up process until the teams have met at each of the charts at least twice and then has the teams talk about all the ideas listed on the charts and clarify any ideas that are unclear at this point.] We have a lot of ideas here to examine even though we have only spent less than 30 minutes on the activity. Let's now go through each chart and make sure that we have an understanding of each idea before we trim the lists down so that we can finalize our decision on these elements."

Pyramid Brainstorming

Even though this idea seems simple, it can have a powerful visual impact on a group's ability to generate lots of ideas. The facilitator explains the power of visual tools in helping to generate ideas, then gets the group involved in the activity. Here are some thoughts to keep in mind as you implement this strategy:

♦ Explain the process of brainstorming to group members and how making a pyramid will help them think creatively.
♦ Be sure the chart paper you are using is large enough to make the pyramid so you can capture all the ideas. You may want to use several charts connected together to give you plenty of room to write the answers in the pyramid shape.

♦ As the group generates an idea, put it on the top. When the second idea is shared, place it in the second row. As new ideas are listed, write them so that the base of the pyramid gets wider. (For example, in the second row, two ideas would be listed; in the third row, three ideas should be written down, and so on) Continue the process until you form a pyramid.

♦ When you start a new row, be sure to let the members know that they should try to fill the row before stopping the brainstorm.

Example

"Today we will be brainstorming ways to help our students do better on the state tests we are required to administer. In order to help open up our thinking, we will engage in a process called pyramid brainstorming. By making a visual chart, it will free up your thinking and help you generate more ideas. Let's get started. [Group generates ideas and the facilitator writes the ideas in a pyramid manner, working down and filling in the rows as new ideas are shared.] We are just at the start of the fifth row. When we have the row filled in, we can take a break from brainstorming. [Group generates four new ideas and fills in the row.] Now that we're finished, let's take some time to clarify the ideas generated. I'll point out each idea. If you have a question, we'll direct it to the person or group that generated that idea. [Facilitator takes the group through clarification.]"

Box 4

This brainstorming technique works on the principle of building on related ideas. The facilitator writes the first concept that needs to be brainstormed on a chart, then lists related topics on other, smaller charts. The idea in this activity is that the group brainstorming adds one idea to the base chart, then adds ideas to the related charts, one at a time. In practice, it looks like this:

♦ This activity can be done either as a whole group or with a group that has been divided into small teams.

♦ The facilitator writes the core concept that needs ideas generated on a large piece of chart paper.

♦ The facilitator either generates three or four more related topics or works with the group to generate these ideas. They are written on smaller pieces of chart paper and placed on the wall surrounding the base chart in a box arrangement. The related ideas revolve around the central theme and are connected to it in a manner similar to a mind map diagram.

- ♦ An idea is generated regarding the base concept and then written on the chart.
- ♦ An idea is generated regarding the related concept and written on that chart.
- ♦ One idea is generated around each of the related concepts. Once all of these have an idea represented, the brainstorming cycles back to the base chart. The group rotates around the charts until the group can generate no more ideas.
- ♦ After the brainstorming is complete, the group begins to clarify the ideas generated.

Example

"Today we are going to generate ideas around our problem with student attendance. I'll put the major topic of attendance here on a piece of chart paper. We need to list three or four topics that are related to or are subsets of attendance. [Group talks about ideas related to the main topic; facilitator writes these ideas on smaller charts and places those charts around the main topic in box fashion.] Now that we have our box formed, here is what we'll do. We'll start with our main topic, brainstorm an idea for addressing that issue, and write it on the chart. Then we'll move to our first related topic, parental support, and list a strategy we think could be helpful in addressing that need. We'll generate one idea for each chart until we work our way around the entire chart, where we'll start the process all over. Let's get started."

Variation

In some settings, the facilitator may find that it is easier for group members to brainstorm on one area and complete their brainstorming there before moving on to the next chart. You will need to use your judgment on what will work best for your group as you implement this idea. Ask the members their preference or try it several ways to see what will generate the most productive process for your group.

Around the World

This technique is similar to the basketball shooting game of the same name. In the basketball version of around the world, the shooter is asked to make baskets from a variety of preestablished places on the court. When a basket is made, the shooter advances to the next spot. When a player has advanced to all the stations, this person has traveled around the world. In the brainstorming version of this activity, a team starts from a specific location where a piece of chart paper is posted. When the team writes down at least four new ideas, it can move to the next chart on the rotation. The first team to finish the rotation or advance to the most charts in the preestablished timeframe is declared the winner. This strategy gets team members to quickly get their ideas down on paper and to move to the next chart. It is good for rapid brainstorming of ideas and eliminates the temptation for team members to begin evaluating the responses. Here are the specifics of the activity:

♦ The entire group is presented with several categories in which ideas need to be brainstormed.

♦ Group members are divided into small teams of two or three members.

♦ Each team is given its own unique color of marker.

♦ The different categories to be brainstormed are written on charts and placed around the room.

♦ Teams are placed at each of the charts and told to generate as many ideas as possible.

♦ Teams need to move to a new chart when at least four new ideas are generated.

♦ The first team to move all the way around the world and cover all the charts is declared the winner.

Example

Chris, a facilitator, explained the following to his group: "In our work together today we need to generate ideas around four major topics. They are

1. Possible fundraising sources for our new playground equipment

2. Ideas for themes for Grandparents Day

3. Courses that we could offer during our career day

4. Teacher gifts for American Education Week

"We are going to generate ideas for all four of these needs all at once in order to save us time. We are going to play a game called Around the World brainstorming. [Explains the procedure, divides the group into three small teams, gives each team its own color of marker, has members move around to the four charts until one group finishes.]"

Popcorn/Musical Charts

This activity is a variation of several of the others already introduced in this chapter, but provides the facilitator and the group with an interesting and novel way to get ideas generated by the group. It is best completed by having people randomly move around to the various charts posted in the room. Here are the basic steps involved:

♦ Divide the large group into small teams of three or four people.
♦ Post the charts containing the major ideas to be brainstormed around the room, allowing ample space between charts for movement.
♦ Tell group members that they will start in their base group at their first chart. Each individual should have a different colored marker if possible. As they are writing, you will be playing music in the background. Their job is to get as many ideas listed (as an individual) on their chart as possible before the music stops.
♦ When the music stops, they need to stop writing and move to another chart in the room. Before moving to the next chart, the individual should initial the section completed.
♦ When the music begins again, they need to write as many ideas as possible on the chart. When the music stops, individuals need to stop writing and move to another chart. The process continues until members have had a chance to visit every chart until the facilitator decides that the group has exhausted its ability to generate ideas.
♦ The facilitator can either count the total number of responses by each person and give them some recognition or just count up the total number of responses provided by all the members.
♦ Once the ideas are listed on the charts, they can be clarified and moved forward in the decision-making process.

Example

Ron told the group he was facilitating, "I have listed the major areas where we need to generate ideas on chart paper and have posted them around the room. In order to help us move along quickly, we'll engage in a process today called Popcorn/Musical Charts brainstorming. In this activity, your job is to list as many possibilities as you can on each chart while the music is playing. When the music starts, write as many unique ideas on the chart as fast as you can; when it stops, you need to stop writing and quickly move to another chart. Even though you will be starting out with a small group, you will move to the various charts in the room as an individual. We will keep the process in place until you have had a chance to visit each of the charts in the room once. I've given each of you your own marker color, so we can see how many ideas you have written at each chart. After the process is complete, we will clarify the ideas listed as a group."

Related Ideas

This brainstorming is related to some of the others that have been highlighted in this chapter, but involves having your group add to its list by generating ideas that are related to the major themes that have been identified on the brainstormed list. Here are some general ideas that need to be considered by the facilitator in implementing this brainstorming strategy:

♦ Once the initial list of ideas is brainstormed, the themes of major topic areas present need to be identified or drawn out. This can be done by the facilitator or by the group itself.
♦ One of the categories that either contains a few ideas or seems to hold potential for expansion is identified; the facilitator identifies this area for further consideration.
♦ Once a list of new ideas is generated, the facilitator stops the brainstorm or moves the group to brainstorm a new category area.
♦ After the group members have generated a good number of ideas, they move into the clarification/evaluation phase of the discussion.

Example

Laurie said to the group she was facilitating, "Now that we have a good list of ideas, let's stop and examine what we have generated for possible ideas. [Group looks and holds a brief discussion.] We have generated ideas in about four general categories. We will reengage in the brainstorming procedure now but focus only on ideas that directly relate to Items 1, 5, and 8 on our list, staff development ideas related to beginning the year. [Group generates four or five more staff development programs that could benefit teachers as they begin the school year such as classroom management, parental communication, and building community.]"

SUMMARY

Brainstorming can be an exciting way to get lots of ideas generated by a group and a good way to help team members learn how to suspend their opinions as they are sharing possible solutions for problems. As powerful as brainstorming can be, keep in mind the following to ensure your success with the process:

- Be sure to frame the process as the facilitator before you get the group started with brainstorming. Be overt in giving the directions, and follow up on what you want the group to do as a result of your brainstorming process.
- Be positive and encouraging during the process. Many group members have not ever experienced an open brainstorming session like what they are about to be involved in. Act as a cheerleader to keep the group energized.
- If group members start to make comments or judge the ideas being listed, remind them that they will be able to evaluate the ideas later. Their job now is to get lots of ideas listed in order to have good depth to consider.
- Be sure to clearly stop the process when the group members have generated a good list of ideas and then move them into the clarification process. As they clarify, make sure that they ask clarifying questions rather than judgmental questions.
- Reinforce the group members for their efforts; help them to see how much they have accomplished.

Reaching the Goal 7

Do what you can, with what you have, where you are.

—Theodore Roosevelt

Act as if it were impossible to fail.

—Dorothea Brande

Most groups have some kind of goal or task that has caused the members to be organized into a team. It's the job of the facilitator to help the group reach its assigned goal. This task is not always as easy as it may seem; there are many factors that can work against teams actually reaching their goal. In this chapter, I highlight some of the factors working against teams being successful in reaching goals and some of the strategies designed to overcome these factors. Review the following focusing questions to help guide your learning in this chapter:

- What do teams do that gets in the way of being successful in reaching their goals and tasks?
- What do leaders do to teams to negatively impact their success?
- How can the work of teams be structured to make them more successful in reaching their goals?
- What strategies can facilitators use to increase the chance of success of a team?
- What structures and templates can help teams be successful in their operation?

THE PROBLEM WITH GOALS

Goals can be wonderful for teams or problematic in their implementation. Here are some of the problems with goals and teams:

- ◆ The team lacks ownership for the goals.
- ◆ The goals given to the team lack specificity.
- ◆ The leadership continues to change or adjust the focus of the goals.
- ◆ The goals are lacking a "stretch" component.
- ◆ The goals are perceived by the team as too aggressive or out of reach.
- ◆ There are too many goals being addressed by the team to provide a clear focus.
- ◆ The team believes that the goals will never be implemented even if it is successful in reaching them because of leadership issues.
- ◆ The goals given to the team are too large and not broken into steps or parts.
- ◆ The goals given to the team have no way of being measured.
- ◆ The team knows that there are no internal resources in place to help the goals be successfully implemented.
- ◆ There is a lack of consensus around the importance of the goals or task; a lack of consensus also exists around the best ways to work on the goals.
- ◆ The goals do not build on team strengths.

These and many other reasons work against teams successfully engaging in and reaching goals. We examine several of the ideas listed above in more detail in this section.

TYPICAL ISSUES INHIBITING GOAL IMPLEMENTATION SUCCESS AND FACILITATOR IMPLICATIONS

Team Ownership

The issue of goal ownership is crucial to success in this area. People don't like to work on goals for which they have no ownership or stake in seeing implemented. It is important that the group that will be impacted by the outcome of the goals be involved in some aspect of helping the team reach the goals.

Facilitator Implications

Obviously if the team is involved in setting the goals, it will be committed to working to make sure the goals are accomplished. Sometimes this is not possible. If the team lacks natural interest or investment in the goals, the facilitator needs to find ways to help the team members connect to it. This can be accomplished by engaging the team members in discussions about the goals, increasing their understanding of what is contained in the goals, and start to develop a personal connection to them. This process builds on some of the work of Peter Senge in *The Fifth Discipline* (1994). I have done this with groups using the following steps:

- Write the goals on chart paper.
- Have group members meet in teams of three or four; assign each team one of the goals to provide more clarity on it for the larger team.
- Have each of the small teams develop a definition that illustrates its understanding of the goal, how it would look, feel, and sound, if it were to be implemented.
- Once the above attributes are identified, have each of the small teams either present its findings to the larger group or post its findings in a gallery. Ask the group to process the information generated by these teams and identify points of agreement and disagreement.
- Hold an open discussion with the large group about its understanding of the goals.
- Once the facilitator is relatively sure that the group understands the substance of the goals, engage the group in making personal and professional connections to them; have the groups break up into small teams again and use chart paper to capture the group's thoughts if necessary.
- Once the group has identified the personal and professional connections to the goals, move to the personal commitment level. Use the same strategies with the group that were used in earlier steps of this process.
- Check with the group to make sure members are moving along together in their understanding, personalization, and commitment.

The steps listed above may seem simple, but implementing this process with a group may be complex. It may take a period of time to bring group members along in the process. Here's how it worked with a group that was recently helped to build commitment to a set of goals:

Recently John was asked to help a group of teachers to set professional goals for their growth, based on a set of national teacher standards. He took the five standards and wrote each on five different sheets of chart paper. He posted the five charts around the perimeter of the meeting room. He divided the larger team into five teams. Each of these teams was given 5 minutes to discuss a goal, write a short phrase defining it, and identify how it would look, sound, and feel if it were implemented in its classroom. All the members were involved in a carousel brainstorming activity to see what the original group wrote, and were told to add their own unique contributions to the original work. Once this task was completed, each team reported the progress of its work. After each presentation, the larger group was engaged in dialogue about the perceptions of the accuracy of the subgroup's work.

Once there was agreement, the small teams examined their connection to each of the goals using the same format. He did this by asking individuals to think about components of the goals that they were already implementing and listing those areas where they could continue to grow in each of the goals. Teams of three met to discuss the existing strengths and future growth potential in each goal area. Finally, the teams were put back together into the large group to talk about the total commitment to the goals. Because the larger group had built an understanding of and a connection to the goals, it was able to connect with the goals as well. The larger group was successful in working with these five goal areas and was able to integrate the principles of the goals into its professional growth-planning processes.

In this example, John took the time to build the understanding, connection, and commitment to the five goals, and the group was successful in its attainment. Even though it took time to build the commitment, the time invested was recaptured during the implementation phase of the project in the past. Before implementing this strategy, John found that when he moved other groups into working on goals, the groups would get started right away, but their enthusiasm would fade part way through the process. With this process, they started more slowly than in the past but were more successful in their task accomplishment.

In summary, the steps used in this example were as follows:

♦ Present the goals statements in a visual form.
♦ Ask the group to deepen its understanding of the goals.
♦ Ask the group to define its connection to the goals.
♦ Ask the group to state its commitment to the goals.
♦ Begin the work on implementing the goals.

Goal Specificity

When goals are written to be very general in nature, they are neutral enough to be protected from attack by any one party, but they become disempowering to the teams assigned to make them happen. Here are some examples of goals that may have been written to make them palatable stakeholders but difficult for teams to implement:

♦ In our district, we will value all learners.
♦ At Roosevelt School, we believe in lifelong learning.
♦ We want to make our program pertinent to all learners.
♦ We serve the needs of our community.
♦ Our team needs to make a decision that will protect learning in the district.

All of these examples are obvious in their lack of the specifics that a team would need to be successful in working on them as a task, but in reality, these kinds of situations are common in organizations. To avoid these kinds of general goals, keep these ideas in mind when generating goals or goal statements:

♦ List a general umbrella or global goal statement.
♦ Visualize how things in the building or district will be different if this general statement is accomplished.
♦ Prune this list down to its core components or critical elements.
♦ Add the components generated to the original goal statement.
♦ Examine the new goal statement to see if it illustrates the scope or the intent of the goal.
♦ Prune it down so it includes crucial information but is not cumbersome.

Facilitator Implications

The facilitator may need to work with the leadership or the team members to clarify goals. It may also be necessary for the facilitator to clarify the goal statements for the team in order to help it to be successful.

Shifts by Leadership

In organizations, change is a constant. At times, the quick pace of change can negatively impact groups working to accomplish goals. If the leadership in a building or district continually changes the language or focus of a goal, there could be serious problems in its implementation. Even minor shifts in the language or focus of a goal statement can send some groups into a tailspin in their efforts to accomplish a goal. We have all experienced educators saying that a goal or topic does not apply to them if they are not specifically named in the process. If the leaders responsible for providing the charge for the team do not have the goal stabilized before transferring it to the team, they set the group up for failure.

Facilitator Implications

The facilitator needs to engage with the leader of the group or organization who has charged the team with accomplishing the goal and help this person to stabilize a goal as much as possible before taking it to a team for implementation. If the goal is still evolving, the facilitator may need to spend time with the leadership to focus the goal as much as possible. Here are some strategies that have been used by facilitators to focus or stabilize goals for both leaders and teams:

- ♦ Engage the leaders in a discussion of the present state of the goal, letting them know about the need for clarity; focus them on specificity and the exact needs of the organization.
- ♦ Put the goal in a visual or picture form; this will help people to see what is desired.
- ♦ Help the organization design an umbrella or overview goal statement; use the members of the organization to define the specifics of the umbrella; take the specifics generated by the team back to the leaders to test their ideas for alignment to the general goal umbrella.
- ♦ Work with the leadership to postpone the goal release until it has been clarified; it may be better for the organization to take a little longer in examining the goal than rushing it out before it has been clarified.

Some facilitators represent the goal in a written manner, while others use a visual format such as mind mapping to ensure that the leader sees the need to focus the goal. The facilitator has to either help the leader discover the need for goal focus or tell this person about the importance of focus. Without a clear, stable goal, it's hard for a team to be successful in its assignment.

The "Stretch" Component

In his book *Masterful Coaching* (1995), Robert Hargrove identifies "the stretch" as one of the most important components needed to motivate teams to reach their goals. If the goal is easily within reach, why is a team needed to attain it? A goal should be just beyond the easy reach of a team but not so far out that it cannot be accomplished. Teams or leaders need the stretch to help them get motivated and turn on their creative problem-solving energies.

Facilitator Implications

If possible, facilitators should always have teams examine goals for understanding and commitment. Facilitators also need to have the team members analyze the gap between the present level of operation and the new skills required to attain this goal. In this process, goals can also be analyzed to make sure there is a level of stretch to motivate the team. Use the following points when asking teams to engage in this examination:

♦ List the goal statement.
♦ Visualize what the organization will look like, feel like, and sound like when this goal is accomplished.
♦ Have team members list the skills that will be needed by the team or organization in order to accomplish the goal.
♦ Have team members list the existing skills possessed by the team or organization.
♦ Point out or have the team identify the gap between the existing and needed skills.
♦ If the skills needed are already in place, the task or goal will not stretch the group.
♦ Have the team reevaluate the goal and its purpose.

Once a team has examined a goal, it can determine the amount of stretch that will be required in order to reach it. The key here is to have goals that are just a little out of reach but not impossible to attain in order to assess the gap between present levels of functioning and the new behaviors that will be required to reach the goal. If the gap is too large or too narrow, the goal attempt may fail. Once the gap has been identified, the team has to make an honest assessment of its ability to fill the skill gap needed to be successful with the goal. A facilitator can help the team make this assessment. If a goal is too easy, it needs to be expanded to provide the motivation the team will need to attain it.

Goals That Are Too Difficult

An opposite problem than what is discussed above happens when a goal is too hard or difficult to be accomplished by a team. This can have the net effect of turning a team off to the goal. The difficulty of a goal can be assessed by examining the gap between the present and future levels of operation under the goal statement. A large performance gap would require those working on the goal to retool their skill set. If a team assesses that the members of its organization will need to be completely retooled in order to accomplish the goal, it may be too difficult.

Facilitator Implications

When facilitators encounter a team that has been assigned a goal that is too difficult to reach, its members need to find a way to make the goal less difficult or complex. Facilitators can accomplish this by

- Asking the team leader to lower the difficulty or comprehensiveness of the goal
- Asking the team leader to break the goal into smaller parts
- Engaging the group in breaking the goal into smaller parts
- Assisting the group in building personal understanding of the goal (as was presented earlier in the Team Ownership section of this chapter)
- Providing scaffolding to assist the team in making the transition from their present level of understanding to the new level needed to be successful with the goal. In providing a scaffold, the facilitator uses existing knowledge or strengths to hold up the team while its members are learning new skills or behaviors

In the following example, the facilitator uses scaffolding to assist the group in accomplishing a complex goal.

Shelly was working with a team to complete a complex, multistep goal. In looking at this goal, she reflected on the strengths and limitations of the team and thought about a strategy to help the members use another successful experience they had in the past to accomplish their present task. In opening the session with the team members, she reviewed their past accomplishment and pointed out how they attacked it. She wrote the two strategies the team had used to be successful in the past and then posted them on the wall. As the members began to work on the new goal, Shelly referred them back to the charts to remind them of their past successful strategies. This assist was just what the team needed to overcome the difficulties the new goal had presented.

In this example, the scaffold was the charts that contained the strategies used in the past. Shelly was able to use those experiences to support the team while it was learning the process that the new goal required.

The Number of Goals

It is common sense that limiting the number of goals a team is asked to accomplish increases its chance of success. Mike Schmoker, an authority on helping teams get results in improvement efforts, writes in *The Results Fieldbook* (2001), citing Fullan and Hargreaves, "Many of the schools tackle only one or two achievement goals annually to prevent the overload that is clearly the enemy of improvement" (p. 37).

Most teams have difficulties when they are given too many goals to accomplish. Focusing on one or two goals at a time seems to be the best for teams.

Facilitator Implications

The facilitator of a group needs to analyze the number and complexity of goals a team is charged to accomplish. When an excessive number has been delegated to a team, the facilitator needs to help narrow the focus. Some facilitators will meet with the leader of the team to negotiate a smaller number. Other facilitators are able to stage the implementation of goals in a plan that allows the team to attack one or two at a time before moving on to address others. Still other facilitators point out to the team the situation and ask the team to prioritize its focus so that it is working on only one or two goals at a time. Whatever the strategy, when it is focused on just a few goals, the team has more success with the process.

Belief by the Team That the Goal Cannot or Will Not Be Implemented

If the team has no confidence that the goal will be implemented, there is no reason to engage the team in the process of working on the goal.

Facilitator Implications

The facilitator needs to make sure that the goal is something that has or will have the commitment from leadership to be implemented. A candid discussion on this topic is essential for the success of the team. Some facilitators help team leaders by asking a set of questions about the goal and the implementation process to help leadership see all the components that are required for a goal to be successfully implemented. Their questions include the following:

- ◆ "What are you looking for from this team as it works to accomplish the goal you have given it?"
- ◆ "What are your plans after the team members have finished their work?"
- ◆ "What resources will be needed to implement their suggestions?"
- ◆ "How will you acquire or reallocate those resources?"
- ◆ "What possible solutions could this team design that you would be in support of implementing?"
- ◆ "What possible solutions could this team design that you would not be in favor of implementing?"

The answers provided and the reactions of the leadership give a facilitator an indication of whether the efforts of the team will be supported by the leadership or cast aside. From this point, the facilitator needs to determine whether or not engaging the team in the task is worth the time and effort needed to produce the solution. If the facilitator has a choice, it is better not to engage the team in the goal.

OTHER IMPORTANT CONSIDERATIONS FOR SUCCESS IN THE GOAL PROCESS

The Role of Vision in the Goal Process

Vision has a definite role in setting and reaching goals for a team. In the past, leaders were required to develop the vision and impart it to the other team members. In today's environment, it is important to develop a shared sense of vision as a group or team.

In *The Fifth Discipline Fieldbook* (1994), Peter Senge shares this story that underscores the importance of shared vision:

When Czechoslovakia became a democracy almost overnight in 1989, one of the first tasks for the new leaders was planning elections. They could have designed five- or six-year terms, enough to re-create the new country's institutions. But instead, they set the terms at two years—barely enough time to draft a constitution.

As Vaclav Havel, the writer and former dissident who was elected President, explained later:

"We found ourselves at a transitional period, when everything [was] being reborn. . . . The idea of democracy [had] won in every respect, but the outcome was not yet a genuine, fully fledged democracy."

Havel had plenty of ideas about what the country should do, but he recognized the dangers of imposing a vision, no matter how worthy, on the country from above. Instead, he and Czechoslovakia's other leaders developed strategic mechanisms to involve the country as a whole in developing its future: referendums, public meetings, support for new political parties, and extensive discussion on radio.

The leaders knew they would vehemently disagree with some of the results—such as Slovakia's choice to secede. "Yet the decision," Havel argued, "is entirely up to Slovakia." In the end, the two years spent building shared vision didn't solve many problems itself; but it created a environment in which the people believe they were part of a common entity—a community. The new Czech Republic is credited with having the most vibrant national atmosphere in Eastern Europe today. (pp. 297-298)

When I work with teams, I usually read this short story to them so they understand the purpose of building shared vision. In most cases, it has helped the group to take the process seriously and to develop a clear and focused vision for their task.

The idea of a shared vision helps teams in the following ways:

1. Lets them see the final product

2. Develops ownership for the goal

3. Provides the criteria for assessment

When group members are clear about their goal, they are able to use their goal statements as a form of assessment. Group members can benefit from actually writing out what their vision is for the final product if the goal they are working on is successfully implemented. Let's look at two examples:

1. In setting a goal to expand student academic offerings, a team develops the following vision for the completion of its task:

♦ Student needs and interests will be considered in developing the new offerings.
♦ The new course offerings will be comprehensive in their scope.
♦ The plan developed will be tailored to address the needs of all students.
♦ The new course offerings will build upon the strengths of the school.

2. Another team is working to adopt a new text series for an elementary school. The group sets a goal to choose a series that does the following:

♦ It integrates ideas to work with students who have multiple learning styles.
♦ It builds on the existing strengths of the staff.
♦ It offers a multisensory approach to learning.
♦ It has follow-up materials available.
♦ It offers multiple assessment options.

In both of these examples, you'll notice that the vision of the group revolves around the final product. By being very specific at the onset, these groups will be able to use the ideas generated in their initial visions to assess their success with the process. In some settings, facilitators have their group establish a shared vision around how the group will operate. In other situations, the shared vision has been generated around more generic outcomes.

Team Benefits of Developing Shared Goal Vision

1. **It builds excitement.** Teams enjoy dreaming together. By working as a group to generate a shared vision for the process, a certain amount of excitement is built.

2. **It helps to break the goal into parts.** Once the team has built a vision for its final product, it is easy to go back and fill in the various steps or parts that need to be put in place for success. This is a key component of using vision to help reach a goal.

3. **It provides a map.** It allows the team to actually see what the finished product of its work might be.

4. **It personalizes the goal.** Each team member is able to understand his or her unique contribution to the success of the process.

Working with goals can be a rewarding situation or one that stalls a team in its task. As a facilitator, be sure to spend some time helping the team to understand and use the goal process to its advantage.

Break the Task Into Small Parts

It is much easier for people to get a task completed if they break it into small, accomplishable parts. As their facilitator, you should initially decide how to break the task down. For some content areas, the parts are dependent on each other, while in other situations, the parts are independent of each other. Take this into consideration when breaking the content down. Some facilitators take the content and represent it in its component parts using some type of visual.

Three examples of how facilitators have broken goals into small parts visually are represented in Figure 7.1. In using these visual representations to help a team to see how a goal was broken into steps, the facilitators actually drew these figures on a piece of chart paper, then involved the teams they were facilitating to generate the subgoals in each of the steps where the word *Part* is currently listed. The examples in Figure 7.1 illustrate goals with only three subparts; in reality you may need to design a visual that contains a different number of subgoals to fit the needs of your group.

Figure 7.1

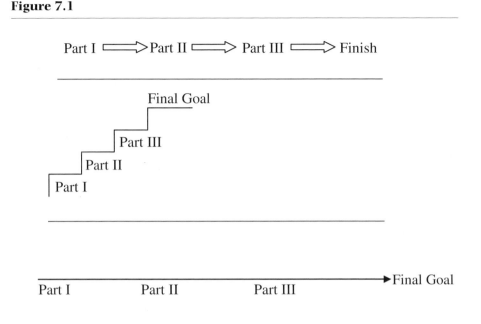

Setting Parameters for Each Part of the Decision

Within some tasks there exists a high level of complexity. Because of this complexity, it may be hard for some groups to see the end in a process. If you analyze their task and identify specific parameters for each part of the process, it can assist them in reaching the final portion of the task. Here are some examples of this strategy in action:

1. I was working with a group recently that needed to make a decision about the projects a community was going to work on during the next year. The group had selected three projects that needed to be considered. Each of the projects had its own set of limitations. We looked at each idea, listed the limitations on a piece of chart paper so they were visible to everyone, and then prioritized each idea based on its limitations and possible contributions to the community. This process was very helpful in getting the group to move forward in its decision-making process. As the ideas were discussed in the group, the group was able to see the limitations and how the solutions generated could help to make some of the ideas work in our unique situation.

2. In another situation, I was working with a team that was interested in implementing a literacy project across the school district. The success of this project depended on several variables, including

the coordination of local assistance agencies, the alignment of the district language arts curriculum, and the cooperation of the local library board. As a team, we listed the factors needed for success and the possible restrictions for each of the factors. We then brainstormed a way to impact the factors to move in a positive direction and assigned one team member to follow up with the community agencies—one to work with the curriculum alignment process, and a third to work with the library board. This division helped us break the total task into parts, kept us posted on the progress of these different groups, and allowed the original team to move forward on the agenda it was charged to implement.

By breaking the larger task down into parts, team members were able to see how all the factors in the situation could work together for success. Breaking the task down also helped our team to chip away at some of the problems that would hold back success in the initial stages. This approach helped the team members take on issues only when needed as they prepared to implement the goal they had been assigned.

Dependent Versus Independent Variables in a Decision

At times, teams can get hung up on small details when trying to put together decisions. These teams can think that certain components are required for the success of a project, when in fact they may have nothing to do with the immediate problem. It is important for these teams to look at the entire program or decision and flush out those items that are dependent on each other for success and those that are independent of each other for success. Some facilitators use a chart or template (see Table 7.1) to help them with this problem.

By charting these ideas, the team may be able to move forward on those issues that are not dependent on other variables first, get the variables addressed that may be holding up progress, and finally address dependent variables. By breaking the process down into achievable parts, the success of the group is enhanced.

Setting Time Limits for Each Part of a Task

Sometimes, a group can be energized by constraining the time it has available to complete a portion or segment of a task. People tend to work hard when starting a new task, so the idea here is to take a large task, break it into parts, and give the group a chance to have several new starts within the same large project. Let's look at some examples of how this has worked with real groups.

Table 7.1

Decision/program component	This component is dependent on . . .	This component is not dependent on . . .

A high school curriculum team was working to decide possible course offerings for the upcoming school year. The group was operating at a low energy level because of the depth and complexity of the task facing it. The facilitator, Roxanne, decided to break the task down and set time limits for each portion of the task. She set up the following schedule:

- 3:00-3:10   Listing of student needs and interests in the building
- 3:10-3:30   Brainstorming of course offerings to meet these needs
- 3:30-3:40   Clarification of brainstormed list, development of a cost-benefits chart
- 3:40-4:00   Prioritization of solutions/course offerings
- 4:00-4:15   Final clarifications
- 4:15-4:30   Final decision on course offerings

By breaking the task at hand into parts, Roxanne was able to keep the group focused and on track in order to make a decision. This group had been notorious in the past for getting off subject and for letting the members' emotions drive their discussions. By keeping them on the time schedule, she moved them through the process and helped them make a decision based on the needs of students rather than their own personal preferences.

The Use of Language Tools to Help
Groups Successfully Implement Their Goals

In her book *The Gentle Art of Verbal Self-Defense* (1993), author Suzette Elgin discusses the principle of presuppositions. In general, presuppositions act as tools to help facilitators plant positive seeds in the minds of their team members. These presuppositions communicate directly with the subconscious part of the minds of team members and help make them successful in the goal process. Presuppositions are used when giving directions or when clarifying tasks to help plant the seeds of success. For example, when giving a team directions, the facilitator could say, "As we work together to solve this problem . . . " This subconsciously communicates that the facilitator believes that the group members will be successful with the task by working together. In relation to the goal attainment process, the following positive presuppositions have been used by facilitators to help team members:

- "As you move forward to solve the problem of . . . "
- "When you return to your school tomorrow, what is one thing you will start with to begin the implementation of . . . "
- "As you work through the difficulties, what strategies will you use to . . . "
- "Now that you have been energized, how do you plan to transfer this energy to the implementation process?"
- "What resources and assistance will you be providing to others who are . . . "
- "In moving forward to support each other, what will be your first step in the implementation process?"
- "What kinds of assistance will you provide your team as . . . "

In all these examples, the language that is communicated to the team members both consciously and subconsciously connects with them and empowers their problem-solving capacities. Given the fact that members eventually learn to talk like this with each other as well, the mind-set of the group becomes positive rather than negative. Many groups over the years have accomplished more than they were originally capable of doing as a result of the facilitators, by using positive presuppositions in their directions and clarification statements to these groups, establishing the belief that the groups could do the job. Positive presuppositions serve teams by helping to set up those kinds of positive thoughts and expectations.

Consensus in the Goal Process

Teams use consensus to build ownership for their goals and their implementation. While much has been written about consensus, the core of it relates to getting a team to agree to try out an idea for a time to see if it has merit. The members also agree not to engage in efforts to actively sabotage the idea in its initial implementation. Consensus benefits teams by

- ♦ Allowing the team members to have a dialogue over an issue and make sure all points are clarified before moving on to a decision
- ♦ Assessing the relative support for an issue and using this information to make decisions about what will be needed in the implementation stage to make the effort a success
- ♦ Helping a team to avoid voting blocks or power plays in its decision-making process
- ♦ Allowing win-win solutions to decisions being considered by the team

Types of Consensus Processes

There are many processes for a group to use in reaching consensus. In this section, I highlight several that seem to work with decision-making teams.

Hand Consensus. In this type of consensus process, team members show their relative support for an issue through holding up a number of fingers from zero to five. A zero vote means that they will work to undermine the decision; a vote of five means that they will totally support the decision. Normally, the facilitator works with the team to establish a threshold number under which a decision does not get moved forward. In general, the process works like this:

- ♦ The team considers a variety of ideas in relation to a decision or problem.
- ♦ The list of possible ideas is narrowed to one or two possibilities.
- ♦ A member of the team makes a motion for an idea or solution to be moved forward in the decision-making process.
- ♦ Group dialogue occurs around the proposal.
- ♦ The group members are asked to indicate their support for the proposal by holding up one to five fingers.
- ♦ If all the team members hold up more than three fingers (the threshold established by the team), the proposal is adopted; if any

members hold up three or less fingers, the team must find out what factors are keeping them from supporting the proposal and help clarify their concerns.

♦ If the concern can be addressed, the proposal is moved forward with another consensus signal; if the concerns cannot be addressed, the proposal is either dropped or adjusted so that the concerns can be addressed.

Thumb Consensus. This process is similar to the hand method, but team members are asked to indicate their agreement using only three possible signals:

1. Thumbs up: "I agree with this idea"

2. Thumbs down: "I disagree with this idea"

3. Thumbs to the side: "I need more information before committing either way"

The decision-making procedure involves the following steps:

♦ The team narrows its list of possible solutions to one or two ideas.
♦ A member of the team makes a proposal to the team stating the desire to have the idea or strategy placed under consideration by the team.
♦ Members discuss the proposal or idea, and they seek clarification of the major points in the proposal.
♦ The originator of the proposal calls for a signal of the members' preference; if members signal "no" or "more information needed," they are asked to state their discomfort with the proposal. The team works to address those concerns.
♦ Once all the concerns have been addressed, the proposal is moved forward.

Point Consensus. In this method, each member is given a number of points to assign to possible ideas. Each member is allowed to assign the points to the ideas being considered for solution. The ideas with the most points are chosen as the ones that are moved forward in the process. This strategy works like this:

♦ A number of possible ideas are talked about by the team; the ideas that seem to have the most merit are written on a piece of chart paper. Each team member is given a set number of voting chips (these can be anything that will hold a place and that will stick to the chart paper such as paper clips, sticky notes, stars, or stickers).

◆ Once all the ideas have been clarified, team members are given a set amount of time to place their points on the chart next to their choices.
◆ At the end of the point placement period, the facilitator counts the points. The idea gaining the most support is moved forward.
◆ In some cases, teams use this process as a narrowing activity and then engage in a more thorough discussion of the "narrowed ideas."

Team Huddle. At times, it can be difficult for a team to talk about an issue and work toward consensus in an open forum in a meeting. For these times, facilitators have used a concept called Team Huddle. In this strategy, team members break into small groups to openly talk about the issues related to their decision. It works like this:

◆ Once the facilitator notices that dialogue around the clarification of an issue or a series of issues is becoming difficult, the facilitator calls for a huddle.
◆ Team members are divided into small groups to talk about the issue or issues in more depth.
◆ A short time is set aside for the huddle; the facilitator gives the small groups very specific assignments to complete during the huddle period (e.g., "Talk about the time commitments required for each of the possible solutions or work through the negative feelings that may be associated with each of the proposed ideas").
◆ At the end of the huddle period, each group is given a chance to report on the ideas it discussed in the huddle; the large team reacts to the ideas that are shared, and those ideas that have merit are discussed in more depth or adopted by the large team.

The facilitator in the following example used the huddle method to help a group work through issues that had developed in relation to scheduling its meetings.

In a recent meeting of a task force, Jerry noticed that the members were getting rigid in listening to and accepting ideas that were being shared to establish their meeting schedule for the upcoming year. Several of the members had conflicts and were trying to get only their needs considered in the schedule. Jerry randomly divided the team into three small groups, each consisting of five members. He asked the members to generate possible solutions to the dilemma that fit into the parameters he had placed on the board in the front of the room. Those parameters were as follows:

◆ The solution must fit the needs of the task force, not individual members of the task force.

♦ All members must have an equal positive and negative impact on their personal schedules as a result of the decision.

♦ Each meeting of the task force scheduled must have a membership that reflected the larger groups that the task force members represented.

♦ The final decision must be acceptable to all members of the task force.

The small groups spent some time considering the decision using the parameters outlined by the facilitator. The small huddle groups lowered the anxiety and emotions that had been present on the team before the group was divided into smaller teams. In the end, a schedule was designed that appealed to all members and fit the criteria established by the facilitator.

Delegating Tasks to Others

Decision-making teams and task forces may be involved in setting up a process for solving a problem or in making a decision involving an improvement effort, but many times, the actual work of the project must be completed by others. It is important that these teams are able to communicate the work that needs to be completed. This is the process of delegation. The following checklist has proven helpful in delegating tasks to others:

1. Think through the job assignment; identify all the components needed to do a good job with the assignment.

2. Think about the group that will be doing the task or assignment and identify the skills needed to do the job. Make sure that this group has an opportunity to learn these skills.

3. Meet with the group that will be implementing the plan or ideas. Clearly communicate the plan and all of its subcomponents and timelines.

4. Provide a clear picture of the completed job or task. Have the group members describe this picture in their own words. Provide an opportunity for questions and concerns to be aired. The group needs to go through some of the same thinking processes that the team that originally designed the plan went through before it is ready to develop ownership for it.

5. Teach the group the skills necessary to do the task well.

6. Establish a schedule to check on progress during the course of the task or project.

7. Be sure to provide the team with feedback during its implementation efforts.

8. Design a schedule to provide follow-up and assistance with the idea or project.

Following these steps will help the team ensure that the idea will be successfully implemented and that its time and effort in designing the project have not been wasted.

Follow-Up and Its Impact on the Goal Process

Follow-up is important to the success of the goal process for teams. In follow-up, the team is engaged in revisiting or reviewing key components of the goal or goal-setting experience. They revisit to keep the goal fresh in their minds and to check on the implementation process. Teams find the following points helpful in the process of follow-up:

♦ Schedule regular times to review the goal or check on progress. The schedule is best developed right after the end of the goal-setting process. Talking about the goal on at least a monthly basis seems to work for most teams.

♦ After setting the goal, generate a list of needs or concerns relating to the implementation process. Bring this list to the follow-up meetings; as the team addresses the concerns, cross those items off the list. This process allows the team to see progress toward the successful implementation of the goal.

♦ Make a visual copy of the goal and its implementation process that can be posted in a prominent place. Tell staff about the reason for posting this information and remind them to examine the plan periodically to see if it is being implemented in the proper manner.

♦ In the follow-up meetings, be sure to encourage people to talk about what is going well and what is not going well. It is a good practice to have an open discussion about all aspects of the project. Cross off any concerns that have been addressed on the list that was developed at the beginning of the process. Add any new concerns to this list as well.

♦ Reinforce the team for its progress on the goal. Involve team members in evaluating their own progress.

♦ Set a clear timeline for starting, evaluating, and closing down the goal. Good plans have clear beginnings and clear ends as well. Plan a celebration at the end of the first phase of the goal implementation process.

Many schools have goal-setting templates that can help a team to set and reach goals in school improvement, strategic planning, decision making, and other areas of team operation. If these templates make sense for your team, use them to assist in the planning of your goals. Use the template in Table 7.2 to plan the follow-up for the goal or goals you have

Table 7.2   Goal Follow-Up Template

1. List the goal or goals. Be sure to include any specific strategies, timelines, needs, or other information pertinent to the goal.

   _____
   _____
   _____

2. List the monthly follow-up discussion dates that have been planned to revisit the goal and refine its implementation. Define who will be responsible for calling the meetings and developing the agendas for these meetings.

   _____
   _____
   _____

3. List the needs and concerns that were generated at the start of the implementation phase of the process. How might these needs and concerns be addressed? Make a list with two columns: Needs/Concerns and Ideas to Address.

   Needs/Concerns   Ideas to Address

   _____
   _____
   _____

4. How have people in the organization been notified of the goal or focus? What kinds of visual plans have been posted in the building?

   _____
   _____
   _____

5. How are you planning to hold an open discussion about the positive aspects and the concerns that have not yet been addressed in relation to the goal? What tools will you use to get all ideas and opinions on the table at this meeting?

   _____
   _____
   _____

6. When will the first phase of the goal implementation be finished? What plans are in place for a celebration?

   _____
   _____
   _____

Table 7.3   Goal-Setting Template

General Goal_____

Academic area or area of focus_____
_____

Team members_____
_____

1. General goal statement	2. Present level of functioning	3. Gap between present level of functioning and desired level of functioning	4. Strategies needed to be successful with goal area	5. Timeline for implementation	6. People responsible for strategies or goal area	7. Vision of what school or classroom will look like if the goal is attained

helped your team to establish. The planning template in Table 7.3 has been put together using a variety of sources. If your school or district does not have a good form to use in planning your goals, consider using the one provided in Table 7.3. This template can help a group to visually capture all the planning components in one location and can provide easy access for checking up and maintaining the goal. Many teams have found it to be beneficial in helping them reach their goals.

Groups that have been successful with the goal-setting template typically start out by completing the information in Cell 1, then moving to Cell 7. They spend considerable time generating the vision of the finished goal. Cell 7 helps to build the ownership for the goal and gives the group a picture that can be used to design the assessment strategies that will be used to measure the completed goal. Once Cells 1 and 7 have been completed, the group can now go back and complete the information for the remaining cells. This template is normally very effective if transcribed onto a large piece of chart paper and posted in the meeting room. This allows the group to complete it as a large group and see it being filled in at the same time. Once it is completed, it can also serve as the plan that is posted for the whole group to refer to as it is being implemented.

SUMMARY

In this chapter, I discuss strategies for assisting a team in being successful with the implementation of its decisions, recommendations, and improvement plans. Many teams have spent considerable time thinking through the problems that face their organizations, only to have all their work go to waste because nothing came of it. This is not only disheartening to the team but sets up the rest of the organization to think that nothing really comes of the team's efforts to meet and problem-solve. If this condition is allowed to go on over a number of years, people may become cynical and stop volunteering for teams. When this occurs, one possible source of solution to the problems faced by organizations is closed. Once this happens, the health of the organization begins to fail.

The strategies presented here include ways to follow up to make sure that efforts are reinforced and continue to be supported, ways to effectively delegate plans to others, common implementation problems faced by teams, and strategies to help in setting and reaching meaningful and pertinent goals. All these strategies and the others presented in this chapter help the facilitator work with the team to make its members successful in their efforts to make decisions and improve the learning conditions in their organizations.

Putting On Your Oxygen Mask

People who fight fire with fire usually end up with ashes.

—Abigail Van Buren

When you come to the end of your rope, tie a knot and hang on.

—Franklin Delano Roosevelt

The flight attendants make almost the same announcement every time a plane takes off: "If the cabin pressure should drop while we are in flight, oxygen masks will drop down from the ceiling panel. When this happens, put the mask on yourself first, then put the mask on others around you."

This familiar announcement relates well to the facilitation process. If facilitators can keep thinking and problem-solving during a session, they can devote the attention needed to keep the group on task as well. If facilitators get caught up in the emotions of what is happening in the meeting, the effectiveness of facilitators could be diminished. Facilitators must find ways to keep any negative energy from impacting their performance. This chapter provides strategies to be implemented that keep the group from taking advantage of you and your level of kindness and helps you block any negative emotions or energy from getting to you and impacting your thinking and processing during a facilitation session. Use the following focusing questions to guide you as you read this chapter:

- ◆ Why is there a need for self-protection as a facilitator?
- ◆ How do negative emotions impact your performance as a facilitator?

♦ What is your role in facilitating teams?

♦ How can presuppositions assist you in working with groups?

♦ What merit does reflecting emotions back to the group have for you?

♦ What strategies seem to fit your style and needs?

IMPORTANT FACTORS FOR FACILITATORS TO TRACK

Facilitating a team is a highly emotional activity. Facilitators are spending time tracking multiple aspects as they work with people. Those include

♦ Tracking participation in activities

♦ Watching body language for cues about group emotions

♦ Keeping track of the pace of progress toward the goals of the meeting

♦ Tracking their own language to make sure it moves the group forward rather than holds the group back

♦ Evaluating the maps, strategies, and moves they may want to make to keep the group productive

♦ Monitoring room comforts such as temperature, lighting, and physical space to make sure that team members are working in an atmosphere that is conducive to learning

IMPORTANCE OF SELF-PROTECTION

Tracking all the elements that occur in a meeting can put a huge strain on the mental processing of the facilitator. Since the brain can only successfully track a few ideas or items at a time, it's important that the facilitator is able to block out distracting elements or negative emotions. When people are under stress, their brain concentrates on survival first. It will do what it needs to do in order to survive. When the negative emotions get into the facilitators' brains, their thinking and problem-solving skills can be diminished. The reduction in thinking can make it difficult for facilitators to objectively guide the group toward its task.

This chapter is written to help facilitators find ways to keep the emotions of team members from negatively impacting their thinking when working with a group. The strategies highlighted here can work on their own but are more effective when implemented in tandem with other facilitator strategies. For example, facilitators can clearly frame their role with a team and use a gesture where they point to the team to reinforce the responsibilities of both parties in the meeting. These two strategies work together to reinforce the point of team member and facilitator responsibility.

Table 8.1

Conditions Facilitators Can Impact	Conditions Facilitators Cannot Impact
The conditions established for the meeting	The attitudes the participants bring to the meeting
The pace at which the task is attacked	The task that has been assigned
The tone of the meeting	Past meetings or assignments the participants have experienced
The processing activities the group members are asked to participate in to accomplish the task	The relationships between the participants outside the meeting setting
Making the topic meaningful to the participants	Making the participants follow facilitator advice
Building the connections between group members as the team works together on the project	Socially unacceptable or deviant behaviors exhibited by group members

As you read about each specific strategy in this chapter, be thinking about how you could couple each with another strategy that you've read about in this book or used successfully with a group in the past.

UNDERSTANDING YOUR ROLE AS THE GROUP FACILITATOR

Remember, facilitators serve in a much different role than that of group leaders or supervisors. A facilitator helps a group work together to reach a set of objectives or expectations. There are certain elements that are out of your control as a facilitator. Table 8.1 gives a sampling of those items.

Framing Your Role With the Team

In order to serve a team well, it's important for a facilitator to frame the role. In framing, facilitators leading a meeting draw a boundary around what they can and can't control. This not only helps facilitators in the area of self-protection, but it also helps the group to be more responsible for its own actions. This role explanation doesn't have to be very detailed or lengthy, but clarity is the key. Here are several examples:

1. Tayna, a facilitator, said to her group, "I am happy to be working with you today as your facilitator. I am here to help you work together, but the ultimate decision as a team is totally up to you. I understand this is a slightly different role than I normally serve as a member of this team, but I will not participate in the final decision because I will be concentrating on the group's processing during this session."

2. Mike told a peer group that he was leading, "Our group needed someone to help lead us through the decision-making process on our new science curriculum. I volunteered to lead the committee as a member in order to work with you. I've been told that my job is to keep you going while you are working on this project. As a facilitator, I will not be forcing any ideas on you, but rather I will be putting most of the responsibility for the decision and the processes we use on you."

3. "As your facilitator, it is my job to set up ground rules and make sure this is a safe environment for you to make a decision," said Hal, as he was starting a team meeting. "I didn't decide your task nor do I have any preconceived notion about what is the right answer for your situation. If I perceive that the group is getting negative or bogged down in the process, I'll let you know. I have some processes that will help you to move along on your task so we can finish on time."

USE OF POSITIVE PRESUPPOSITIONS

In her book *The Gentle Art of Verbal Self-Defense* (1993), author Suzette Elgin discusses a communication tool called a presupposition. In general, a presupposition has these characteristics:

♦ They are embedded in the language we use.
♦ They depend on our intonation and inflection for meaning.
♦ They help to plant a seed in the mind of the person receiving the statement to take some action or to develop a certain attitude.
♦ They can act to shift the responsibility from the facilitator to the participants.

Presuppositions can protect a facilitator and make team members more effective because they plant a seed with a group about how the group members will interact in a session. Presuppositions can also help the facilitator to shift the responsibility for the group success from the facilitator to the team members. This ability to shift the responsibility can come in handy when encountering difficult situations or high emotions. When the energy from these situations is directed back to the group members, the facilitator is able to think and keep the group moving in a positive direction. Here are some examples of presuppositional statements where the responsibility has been shifted to the participants:

- "As you think about how you'll work together to do . . ."
- "What are your plans for . . .?"
- "What will you need as you begin to solve . . .?"
- "Share your next steps for . . ."
- "In relation to this situation, what will be the group's first step . . .?"
- "What is your role in . . .?"
- "Share your ideas for . . ."
- "What will you do to address . . .?"

In each of these examples, the facilitator uses the statement to shift the responsibility to the team so that the team owns the problem rather than the facilitator.

Presuppositions also help the facilitator establish a collaborative atmosphere, because they plant the seed for working together. Here are several examples"

- "What ideas could we come up with together to . . .?"
- "How do you see it . . .?"
- "As we work together, . . ."
- "Once you help me understand . . ."
- "We can begin to design . . ."
- "Let's work together to . . ."
- "Your role in this is . . .My role is . . ."
- "In previous situations we have been able to . . . I'm sure we can do . . ."

In each of these statements, the message is clear that the speaker is interested in forming a collaborative relationship or in putting the responsibility where it belongs in the relationship. By constructing the statements in this manner, the speaker communicates with the subconscious mind of the person receiving the message and begins to shift the thinking of that person toward the desired result. Presuppositions can be used for teams as well as for individuals by a facilitator.

Finally, presuppositions can help to build the thinking and problem-solving capacities of the group. In the next set of examples, the statements are designed around developing a specialized thinking skill in team members.

- ♦ "How will you use what you've learned today . . .?" (designed to help person learn transfer of skills)
- ♦ "What did you notice when you . . .?" (helps increase observational/cause-effect)
- ♦ "Tell me more about the . . ." (develops elaboration)
- ♦ "Please explain your thoughts when you . . ." (gets individual to rationalize thinking)
- ♦ "How did you feel when . . .?" (develops emotional responses)
- ♦ "Give me more details about . . ." (designed to deepen detail recall)
- ♦ "What were you trying for when you . . .?" (draws out planning and anticipation skills)
- ♦ "What happened first, second . . .?" (strengthens sequencing)
- ♦ "What did you observe that led you to the conclusion . . .?" (cause/effect relationships, reflections)
- ♦ "How will what you observed impact . . .?" (reflection, future use)
- ♦ "Please replay the most important . . ." (recalling important events, sequencing)

GESTURING

Humans have a wide range of nonverbal communication strategies. Facilitators use their eyes, face, arms, and hands to communicate to their team members. These nonverbal communications function to keep the group engaged and moving toward its objectives. Gestures can also be used to direct energy that is produced in the group. It is important to maintain the proper level of energy, for both the facilitator and the team.

Earlier in this chapter, I mentioned that energy flow impacts the thinking of a facilitator; too much emotional energy can get in the way of effective thinking, while too little energy can cause a group to shut down. The optimal amount of group energy can motivate and keep both the team and the facilitator engaged in the process.

Facilitators find that coupling gestures with other strategies such as pacing their voice and looking into the eyes of their team members helps them reinforce verbal messages or convey a particular thought or emotion to a team. Gestures can also help facilitators block or divert energy away from themselves to help them think while they are facilitating groups. Let's look more closely at gestures and their potential for helping facilitators work effectively with groups.

According to Toastmasters International (1982, p. 9), the premier speakers' support organization in the United States, all gestures can be grouped into one of the following major categories:

♦ **Descriptive gestures.** These are used to clarify or enhance a verbal message. They help the audience understand comparisons and contrasts and to visualize the size, shape, movement, location, function, and number of objects.

♦ **Empathetic gestures**. These gestures are used to underscore what is being said. They indicate earnestness and conviction. For example, a clenched fist suggests strong feeling, such as anger or determination.

♦ **Suggestive gestures**. These are symbols of ideas and emotions. They help the speaker to create a mood or express a particular thought. An open palm suggests giving or receiving, usually of an idea, while a shrug of the shoulders indicates ignorance or perplexity.

♦ **Prompting gestures**. These gestures are used to evoke a desired response from the audience. If you want your listeners to raise their hands, applaud, or perform some specific action, you'll enhance the response by doing it yourself as an example.

Even though the Toastmasters information was designed for public speakers, it has some good points that are useful for meeting facilitators:

♦ Use gestures in a natural manner when facilitating meetings. As people move from activity to activity, making motions with the hands can guide them and get them accustomed to seeing gestures in the meeting.

♦ Gesturing can be used when asking a group to stay focused on a task for an extended period of time. Coupling a gesture directing the group back to the task with an offering of reassuring words will help to calm the group.

♦ Offering empathy through a combination of voice and gesture may help a group know that its plight is understood and keep it from getting angry or anxious. For example, saying, "I understand," while pointing to yourself and then pointing your finger to the group communicates understanding through both verbal and nonverbal means.

♦ When a group seems to be moving too fast toward a decision in a topic area, offering the verbal message "Let's take it a little slower" while using the suggestive gesture of an outstretched palm (hold up) can help the group get its emotions in check and back on track.

♦ If a team seems to be transferring its negative energy to you or transferring blame toward you for something that happened, combining a stop gesture with a verbal comment that you had nothing to do with the situation can keep the negative energy of the group from reaching you.

Common Gestures and Their Impact

♦ Hand held in front of facilitator, palm toward audience = Stop
♦ Arm and hand extended toward group or individual = Refers to group
♦ Hand and arm move toward facilitator, palm toward facilitator = Refers to me
♦ Arm and hand rotated horizontally in a circle = All of us together
♦ Finger pointed = Refers to person or object pointed at
♦ Arm and hand sweep away from body toward chart or other visual = Please refer to this
♦ Hands and arms out away from the body = Welcome and open to ideas
♦ Fingers held in numerical arrangement = Order or position in sequence
♦ Hand out in front, palms held up = Open for suggestions or unsure about information

These gestures are just a few of the many that facilitators use to help maintain group control and protect themselves from the negative energy that groups sometimes generate. If this is an area that interests you, you may consider studying gesturing and nonverbal communication cues in more depth. Watch movies, public speakers, and others to see how they incorporate gestures into their interactions with others. You can't necessarily copy their gestures and make them yours, but you can begin to enhance your own use of gestures in working with groups.

USE OF CHARTS, PAPERS, AND OTHER VISUALS TO DEFLECT ANGER

When you are facilitating a group, all eyes are on you. As a group becomes more emotional or upset, the negative energy associated with these emotions can be transmitted from the group to you. This can cause you to become more stressed and preoccupied with group emotions. This increased level of stress can also reduce your capacity to think and stay on track during the facilitation session. A colleague, Michael Grinder (personal communication, June 1994), recently shared a strategy called Going Visual that can help to deflect some of the emotions that are normally associated with an angry group or person. Here are some ideas that can help you as you work with groups:

Going Visual

♦ Place controversial information on a chart or projected on a screen, and as you present this information, stand off to the side and point to the information. This keeps the group focused on reading and not staring at you.
♦ Give the group controversial information on a handout. Do not hold a handout yourself. Have the group refer to its own copy for questions and more information.
♦ Post ground rules and norms away from your main facilitation spot in the room. If you need to remind people of these during the session, you can stand off to the side and gesture toward them. This keeps the correction you have had to make from negatively impacting you.
♦ When group members share ideas or suggestions, those should also be posted on a chart or projected on a screen. If group members take issue with the suggestions, their emotions won't be transferred to the group that gave the suggestion.
♦ If there is good news or you want to benefit from having any positive group energy directed at you, consider presenting this information from a handout that you hold in front of you. As you present the good information, you will reap the benefits of the goodwill of the group, since the group members will be looking into your eyes as you are sharing this information.

USE OF POSITIONING IN THE ROOM

Consider changing your position in the room periodically to help keep the group focused and on track during your session. Here are some common positions and their normal impact on a group:

♦ **Standing in front**. Facilitator is in charge; emotions should be directed toward the facilitator.
♦ **Standing off to side**. Facilitator is still managing the group, but the group is directing some of its energy toward its members.
♦ **Standing in back**. Facilitator is monitoring the group, but the group is interacting more with itself than with the facilitator.
♦ **Seated with group**. Facilitator is seen as a part of the group.

- ◆ **Seated in back of room**. Facilitator is no longer in charge; group is directing energy and ideas toward its members.
- ◆ **Seated initially but stands during session**. Facilitator is resuming control of the group.

Even though common sense might tell you what positions to take while you're facilitating, nevertheless, be sure to think about your position in the room when working with groups. Even though the ideas shared here work in most situations, you need to evaluate each group to see what will work best to help keep its energy on a maximum level and to help protect you as their facilitator.

DEVELOPING AN EXIT PLAN

Some people who are asked to facilitate groups can experience the negative emotions that the group is emitting as it works through issues. There are times when no strategy can help get a group back on track. It is in these cases that a facilitator needs to have an exit plan developed. An exit plan is a positive way for a facilitator to stop the process, close down the session, and send people on their way. Keep these ideas in mind as you develop the exit plan for a facilitation session:

1. When you are planning a session, explore your options with the person asking you to facilitate the group. Find out from this person if you have permission to stop the meeting and send the members on their way if the group begins to get out of control.

2. Think through the kinds of behaviors that would make a group so difficult to work with that you would need to stop a session. Are your thoughts reasonable? Could you be overreacting? How will you verify that these behaviors are happening?

3. Examine your agenda for the meeting. Are there natural breaks or stopping points that could work well with the group?

4. Prepare yourself for the fact that if you stop the session, the group may try to talk you into changing your mind. The group may also get more angry at you because you are closing the session. Determine how you will deal with this increased pressure.

5. Once you have determined the criteria for closing down the meeting and have thought through all the possible problems associated with this strategy, be sure to plan how you will deliver the message to the group. Be sure to be firm and direct when using this strategy.

REFLECT EMOTIONS/CONTENT BACK TO THE GROUP

Skilled facilitators find that in many groups, the emotions are quite strong. In many cases, group members have had the prior experience where no one seems to understand or is willing to listen to their ideas or concerns. Since their ideas may have fallen on deaf ears in the past, they may become quite upset in your meeting if they sense that they are not being heard. As a facilitator, you will need to keep on constant alert for this situation. This is especially important when working with a difficult group of people. Sometimes the very reason they get hostile is because no one has listened to them or paid attention to their ideas in the past. As the manager of energy within the team, your role as facilitator is to find ways to reflect the ideas shared back to team members so they feel listened to and valued.

Many of us have had practice in a skill called paraphrasing. In paraphrasing, the listener takes in the information a team member presents, processes this information through his or her own mind, and then gives the information back to the sender in a slightly different form than was originally presented. Let's see how this works in the following example:

> In a session being facilitated in regard to an employee recognition program, one of the members states, "We have tried to put together a good program for as long as I have worked in the district, but we keep coming back to the same old certificates and pins." In using paraphrasing, the facilitator says, "I hear you saying that we keep doing the same thing year after year."

In this example, the facilitator added his understanding of the comment to the situation by saying, "I hear you . . ." In working with difficult groups of people, many facilitators have found it to be beneficial to be more direct in their paraphrase or reflection rather than including the "I heard you say . . ." statement. Read the following example and see how the facilitator statement is different in its more directive form:

> In the session being facilitated in regard to an employee recognition program, one of the members states, "We have tried to put together a good program for as long as I have worked in the district, but we keep coming back to the same old certificates and pins." In using a reflecting response, the facilitator replies, "You feel that we keep doing the same thing year after year."

The difference in this response is that the facilitator does not filter the initial statement through his perception before giving it back to the sender. This facilitator acts somewhat like a mirror giving the information directly back to the sender. Many facilitators who have worked with difficult groups have found this more direct, mirror-like response to be much more meaningful and faster at deescalating the anger and emotions that can stifle a team as it works on complex tasks.

There are many types of reflecting statements that can be generated in a facilitation experience. In this section, I focus on the three major types of reflecting statements facilitators use when working with difficult groups: content reflecting, emotional reflecting, and chunking reflecting.

Content Reflecting

In content reflecting, the facilitator is reflecting back what the sender had said, using slightly different wording to help build understanding and meaning. In this type of reflecting statement, the facilitator uses a short phrase, called a stem, to start off the statement. Here are three examples of reflecting stems that could be used to reflect back the content of an individual or a group:

1. "You shared your thoughts . . ."

2. "Your main concern is . . ."

3. "You said . . ."

These stems provide a base on which to build a more complex reflecting statement. As you examine the next examples, look for the presence of a stem and how the facilitator directly reflected the content back to the sender.

1. In a recent session, a facilitator was working with the group to help it generate a list of possible responses to an internal emergency. As the meeting progressed, one of the members said, "I am having a hard time keeping track of all of this information." The facilitator heard this message and reflected back, "This is a complex topic."

2. As a group was working through its response to a state-mandated internal curriculum audit, one of the members said, "The state is picking on us. Our paperwork and curriculum process is up to standard. They seem to be focused on making us go through this silly exercise." The facilitator responded, "Your main concern about this process is the state's motivation for conducting this audit."

In working with teams, especially teams experiencing difficulty, the ability of the facilitator to reflect back the content helps the team members to understand the major issues facing the team. Some facilitators have said that they feel that team members will get angry if they reflect something back that is different from what the sender actually said. This fear has kept facilitators from using reflecting statements to help the team members feel that the facilitator is listening and understands the issues facing this team. In reality, people will directly tell you if your reflection is not accurate. In the example above, a team member might respond by saying, "I am not concerned about the state's motivation; I am concerned about the amount of work this decision will cause us." After analyzing this reply, the facilitator now understands a part of the reason why the team is having trouble with the decision. The facilitator can begin to generate strategies to help this team deal with the problem and get on with the decision.

Emotional Reflecting

In an emotional reflecting statement, the facilitator listens to the comment made by an individual and reflects back the emotion that was contained in the statement. Emotions drive people's behaviors. Facilitators find that they are able to connect with groups by reflecting back the emotions they hear in the comments. The same facilitators also comment that reflecting emotions has helped them to quickly calm down an angry or difficult group. Emotional reflecting seems to work well when combined with the more direct approach that I talked about earlier. As you look at the following reflecting stem examples, note how they use a direct reflecting approach to get the point across:

- "This is upsetting to you . . ."
- "You are feeling stressed . . ."
- "You are frustrated . . ."
- "You are angry . . ."
- "This process has been frustrating for you . . ."
- "The possible solutions have upset you . . ."
- "You are mad . . ."
- "This is confusing . . ."
- "The team is frustrated . . ."

In these examples, the facilitator was direct in labeling the emotions that she perceived the team or individuals were sending. Reflecting stems help the facilitator have a starting point for attaching other language or directly relating to the emotion to be reflected. Examine the following to see how the facilitator working with these teams used the stem to start the reflection and clearly labeled the perceived emotion:

> A facilitator was given the task of meeting with a group of para-professionals and talk with the members about the budget cuts their department would be facing. No specific positions were named in any layoffs, but this group was told that there would be about 10% less staff working in the schools next year. As a meeting progressed, one paraprofessional said, "I've worked in this district for over 20 years. Every year, our group is told that there will be reductions. I'm getting very tired of this." The facilitator responds by reflecting, "You are upset by the way the district is making its decision." The paraprofessional responds, "Yes, I'm very upset."

In this situation, the facilitator was able to correctly label the emotion. He could see the anger actually leaving the participant as a result of his statement. The participant finally felt listened to as a result of his reflecting statement. Even though she was not completely calmed down, her anxiety was lowered enough for her to listen to what the facilitator had to say in regard to the budget reduction process.

Some facilitators wonder what would happen if they selected the wrong emotion and reflected it back to the sender. In my experience, this has not been a problem, because in most cases, the sender has felt comfortable stating the real emotion being felt. A response of "No, I am not upset; I am angry with how things have been handled here in the past" to the facilitator's observation of "You must be upset by this situation" clearly labels the emotion being felt by the team member. Once this statement has been made, the facilitator now knows the exact emotion the participant is feeling. The facilitator can now begin to think of the strategy to deal with this emotion. In the following example, observe how the emotion is clarified by the person feeling it in the meeting:

> A task force comprised of community members, school district officials, and the board of education was working to determine the school site that would be closed as a result of declining enrollment. During this meeting, one of the community members stated, "My grandfather helped build this school, and my parents and I attended it. I'd hate to see it closed." The facilitator responded by saying, "You feel betrayed by this decision." The community member said, "Not betrayed, just ignored."

Chunking Reflecting

At times, difficult groups may not be able to put their finger on the real problem. Members may share a litany of related issues. In this situation, facilitators can use a process called chunking to put the general concerns in a neat package so that the group can see the interrelationships between the concerns. Here are some ideas to keep in mind when using chunking:

♦ Be sure to listen carefully and try to put related items together in the same category.
♦ Once you have heard the concerns, choose a general category to put them in.
♦ Keep in mind that your initial category only provides a package to hold the concerns. It may need to be adjusted based on the response of the group.
♦ When you chunk or lump concerns together, you are providing a way for the group to minimize or compartmentalize its long list of concerns. In some groups, this helps group members see the big picture rather than getting caught up in the details.

Here are some examples of chunking:

♦ "The three major points you made . . ."
♦ "In general, you've . . ."
♦ "Your thoughts revolve around . . ."
♦ "You are focusing on these two items . . ."
♦ "All of your concerns seem to revolve around . . ."
♦ "In thinking back to your situation, these are the main points . . ."
♦ "Your major points seem to be . . ."
♦ "In reflecting on your comments, I see these themes emerging . . ."
♦ "The first point you stated was . . . The second one was . . ."

As you can see, these stems lump together a larger set of statements to help senders see the large picture. In any case, once senders are able to see that the concerns are linked together, it helps to lower their level of anger and anxiety and makes them less difficult to work with on a team or task force.

The following examples illustrate a more complete picture of how a facilitator uses the skill of chunking comments together in providing a good reflection for the person or team that is experiencing difficulties:

1. A facilitator was working with a group of custodians to help the custodians understand new cleaning procedures in their building. Several of the custodians shared their objections to the new ideas,

including statements such as "This will take more time," "We already have a lot of demands on us, and you're asking us to pick up even more responsibility," and "We're the only group that's been asked to do more with less." The facilitator listened to all these comments and responded back, "All the comments I've just heard are focused on workload issues. Let's stop here and take an objective look at the new ideas and the amount of time they will take."

2. In a meeting of a group that was designing a response to the fact that many students were not completing their work, several members of the group were making comments such as "Our children are not responsible," "Parents today are not interested in their children's education," and "We face increasing competition with other entertainment that takes our children away from their work." The facilitator listened to these comments and responded by saying, "In general, you are saying that there are a lot of factors impacting student success. What we need to do today is identify those sources where we can have a positive impact on turning this problem around."

SUMMARY

In summary, we have examined several methods that facilitators can use in working successfully with difficult groups of people. Difficult groups pose a great challenge to facilitators as they try to help these teams move forward in a productive manner. In addition to the strategies and ideas presented here, there are a variety of other ideas that are presented elsewhere in this book that you may find helpful in working with difficult groups of people. Among those are the following:

- Lower the level of difficulty of the task.
- Divide the group into smaller, more productive teams.
- Constrain the time for tasks.
- Open up the time for tasks.
- Have people share in teams of two.
- Break the task into smaller, easier to reach tasks.
- Put the group into a brainstorming activity.
- Use positive presuppositions.
- Use suspension of opinion.
- Ask the group to reflect its thoughts.

As you facilitate difficult groups, keep these strategies in mind so that you can keep your own thinking moving as you help the group think and problem-solve. Not only will they appreciate your efforts, but you will find the facilitation process much more rewarding and enjoyable.

Transforming a Difficult Group

The way I see it, if you want the rainbow, you've got to put up with the rain.

—Dolly Parton

The difficulties of life are intended to make us better, not bitter.

—Anonymous

Many times in our roles we are asked to lead groups through difficult or emotional meetings. These situations and groups pose unique challenges that require a special focus in order to keep them moving toward resolving issues in a positive fashion. Difficult or angry groups can cause us to feel anxious and nervous, lose our train of thought, or even become hostile ourselves. As the meeting leader of a difficult group, it is crucial to have a bag of strategies ready to use when encountering these situations. In this chapter, we explore strategies to help you successfully lead difficult groups through difficult situations.

Use the following focusing questions to guide your learning in this chapter:

- ◆ What are some of the characteristics that make a group difficult?
- ◆ How can framing help to deal with a negative team?
- ◆ What are some behaviors that individuals use to be difficult?
- ◆ What is the role of music in calming people?
- ◆ How can constraining the agenda get a group to be less difficult?

WHAT IS A DIFFICULT GROUP?

Difficult groups come in all shapes and sizes. The definition of what makes a team difficult is in the eye of the person leading one of these groups. The very characteristics that make a team productive in one setting could make it unproductive in another. The comfort level of the leader can also determine if a group is difficult. As you examine the following list of common difficulties, keep your own perceptions and beliefs in mind in determining whether these situations would cause you difficulty if you were to work with these teams.

A Sample of Difficulties Posed by Groups or Teams

In this sample list are some of the typical behaviors faced by facilitators and some fast ways to deal with them. Throughout this chapter are additional methods designed to help with the kinds of behaviors that are listed below:

♦ **Anger.** The group may be angry about its task or the assignment it has been given. Group members may also be upset about the conditions in the district or building. As a facilitator, it is important to work to lower the level of emotions in the group. Possible remedies to lower the group's emotions are reflecting, framing, and allowing the group members to vent before the meeting starts.

♦ **Lack of interest in the task.** The task the group has been given is not motivating to the members. Ways to deal with lack of interest include asking the group to define what is problematic with the task, working with the group to restructure the task, and breaking the task into parts.

♦ **Passive behavior**. Group members do not get actively engaged in the meeting. To deal with this, ask members why they are not engaged in the task. Implement group activities to energize the team. Have people meet in small groups to work on parts of the task.

♦ **Extremely vocal and outspoken behavior**. In this situation, people are emotional and negative about the task. Establish ground rules or help the group members to develop a set of norms for their behavior. Use paper/marker activities to get their thoughts out. Protect yourself with framing and moving the negative emotions away from yourself.

♦ **The group thinks that its efforts won't solve the problem.** Find out where this belief is anchored. Ask the group to identify what it does have control over. The team needs to increase its scope of control over the issue.

♦ **Living in the past**. This is a common affliction that hampers team effectiveness. Have the team members identify how the past impacts their future work. Ask them to put all of their grievances in an envelope and dispose of the envelope in a ritual that symbolizes getting rid of their past issues. List their complaints on a chart and ask the group members how these problems can be disposed of so they don't interfere with their effectiveness.

♦ **Aversion to process**. At times, groups are encountered that have had bad experiences with process meetings. Limit process to clearly needed situations. Tell the group the purpose behind the process for each activity. Acknowledge group members' aversion to process and reassure them that process will be used only when needed.

♦ **Lack of honesty**. A lack of team honesty about issues breaks down the interdependence that is needed for team success. Model honesty and integrity as a facilitator. Ask the group to gradually address the issue of integrity. Develop team norms around honesty. Reinforce team members for self-disclosing on issues.

♦ **Cynicism and sarcasm**. This can occur between a few members or within the entire team. Step in immediately and stop this behavior. It violates the basic trust that is needed to help the team function. Establish ground rules addressing this problem.

♦ **Unwillingness to see problems from multiple viewpoints**. Without multiple perspectives, the possibilities for solutions will be limited. Engage the team in activities like multiple hats or structure brainstorming charts that require ideas to be generated from a variety of views of the problem. Have the team participate in physical team-building activities; debrief these activities to help members see how the solution of problems needs to utilize multiple approaches.

♦ **Impatience**. In this situation, the group is too anxious about getting the work completed. Members may move forward without the necessary information or make decisions without considering all angles of the problem. Tell the team about the importance of taking the appropriate amount of time to make a decision. Involve members in mental team-building activities and other processes that will force them to slow down in their decision making. Establish a timeline that requires the team to break the task into parts.

♦ **Too much patience**. No sense of seriousness or urgency is seen by the facilitator in team members. Establish an aggressive timeline for completion of the task. Engage team members in participation activities. Ask team members to complete a "what if" exercise where they have to project the consequences of their inaction.

PROBLEM PEOPLE

In their book *How to Make Meetings Work* (1993), Doyle and Straus define common problem people or individuals and possible remedies to deal with these situations:

- ◆ **Latecomer**. Comes late to meetings; wants to be caught up on the content.

Possible remedies: Start the meeting on time. Welcome the latecomer, pull up a chair for the person. Focus the meeting away from the door so the latecomer won't be the center of attention. Evaluate why someone might be late. Make adjustments to deal with the possible causes of people being late.

- ◆ **The early leaver**. Drains energy from the group by always leaving early.

Possible remedies: Evaluate why people might be leaving early. Look at the meeting length and topics. Ask participants up front how long people can meet, and adjust the meeting time accordingly.

- ◆ **The broken record**. Keeps bringing up the same topics and ideas over and over.

Possible remedies: Refer back to written information on charts to let the person know his or her idea has been written down and is important. Stop the meeting and let the person explain his or her idea fully to make sure it has been heard by the team. Reflect the content of the idea back to the speaker to let that person know the idea has been heard. Have group members reflect the idea back to the speaker to let the speaker know the idea has been heard.

- ◆ **The doubting Thomas**. Continuously is negative about every idea shared by the group as a possible solution.

Possible remedies: Remind the individual or group that ideas are not ready to be evaluated at this point. After the reminder, correct the individual for evaluating the idea. Remind the person that evaluation will come later. Frame up the expectation that ideas will not be evaluated on their initial exposure to the group.

♦ **The head shaker**. This person constantly gives nonverbal answers to ideas and questions.

Possible remedies: Block out their nonverbal cues so they don't negatively impact your emotions. Concentrate your attention on the head shaker. Point out to head shakers that you notice their head shaking and ask them to verbally comment. Talk with the person privately if the behavior continues over time.

♦ **The dropout**. This person just sits in the back of the room and disconnects from the meeting.

Possible remedies: Walk to the back near the dropout and conduct the meeting from this location. Look at the dropout and ask a question; allow another member to answer the question. Engage the rest of the group in a participation activity and go back and ask the person about the problem. Evaluate the meeting for content and energy.

♦ **The whisperer**. The whisperer is constantly holding sidebar conversations during the meeting.

Possible remedies: Walk over and stand by the whisperers. When others are engaged in an activity, quietly remind the whisperers not to whisper. If several people are talking, remind them that the team needs to focus on the group conversation; it's important for them not to whisper. Have team members stand up. Reshuffle their seating so that the whisperers are not sitting together.

♦ **The loudmouth**. The loudmouth talks too much and too loudly.

Possible remedies: Walk over and stand by the person. Proximity can make these people more aware of their behavior and may quiet them down. Ask the person to help you by taking notes on the chart tablet. Have the person write down ideas on an individual sheet of paper. Talk with the person at a break. Try to communicate that you understand his or her enthusiasm and expertise, but point out the importance of allowing everyone to talk.

♦ **The attacker**. This person launches attacks on others or their ideas in the meeting.

Possible remedies: Physically move between the attacker and the person being attacked. Bring the focus back to the topic and the importance of diversity of ideas. Ask both parties (if two are fighting) to write down their ideas on chart paper so the group can look at the two situations without emotion. Use emotion, content, or chunking reflecting. If you are being attacked, be careful not to look defensive. Thank the attacker for the information and ask the attacker for alternate ideas. If needed, dismiss the group to a break and talk with the attacker privately about the problem or disagreement.

♦ **The gossiper**. The gossiper brings hearsay information to the meeting.

Possible remedies: Try to get the truth out as soon as possible. Let the person know that you will check out the story outside the meeting. Let the person know that the information is not relevant at this point. Use framing to let the person know that the issue will be dealt with when accurate, verified information is obtained.

♦ **The interpreter**. Speaks for others and cuts in at inappropriate times.

Possible remedies: If the person is speaking for others, stop the comment and ask the original speaker if the comment is true.

♦ **The backseat driver:** This person tries to tell the facilitator how to conduct the meeting.

Possible remedies: After this person makes a suggestion, ask the group members for their thoughts about it; if they like it, try it; if not, this will shut down the person. Point out that there are several ways to facilitate a meeting. Ask the person to try your way. Ask the person if he or she wants to facilitate.

♦ **The busybody**. This person is always ducking in and out of the meeting, taking phone calls, and disrupting the meeting.

Possible remedies: Conduct the meeting in the best possible manner. If the person is a key player, get some agreement on what the group should do in this person's absence. Talk to the busybody before the meeting about the problem with his or her behavior. Schedule the meeting for another time to avoid the conflicts that take this person away from the meeting.

♦ **The interrupter**. The interrupter makes comments before others have finished sharing their ideas.

Possible remedies: Stop the person immediately. Use your voice, body, and gestures to stop the interrupter and allow the original speaker to finish. Remind the group members about their norm of allowing all people to speak. Speak to the interrupter privately about the importance of letting everybody speak in a meeting.

The kinds of behaviors that make a group difficult are unlimited. The bottom line is that any behavior that causes the group to have difficulty working together and reaching its objective is problematic. Some session leaders work with groups that are very hostile in nature; others find groups that are extremely resistant to productive problem resolution. In many cases, team members take out their frustrations and anger on their session leader. In working with these kinds of groups, remember that the members' dysfunctions could be deeply embedded and are usually not your fault. Don't take their behaviors personally; you may be the one person who is able to help them work through their problems and become productive.

IDENTIFICATION STRATEGIES

It is crucial to find ways to identify group difficulties as soon as possible in order to begin to develop a strategy to get them under control. If the problems are identified presession, the facilitator can take the time to generate a set of preventative strategies. If the behaviors are identified during the session, facilitators need to find a way to deal with these problems on their feet. Most facilitators have found that their intuition or gut feeling about a group is extremely accurate. Let's take a look at some strategies facilitators use in order to diagnose a difficult group of people.

Pre-Event Strategies

If you can identify the characteristics of a group before you begin your work with the group, you will be ahead of the game. If you are facilitating a group from within your school or district, you may have inside information that can assist you. If not, you may need to do some research before you begin the process. Here is a list of some pre-event identification strategies you might use to gather information about a group before you begin your work with it:

- ◆ Ask others in your building or district about the group.
- ◆ Observe members of the group in their regular assignment or in another setting.

♦ Personally meet and talk with individuals from the group you will be facilitating.
♦ Read the minutes of previous meetings held with this group.
♦ Talk with individuals who supervise members of the group.
♦ Interview the person who has asked you to facilitate this group.
♦ Administer a survey or questionnaire to the group members you have been asked to facilitate.

Remember, not all of these strategies will work in your situation, but one of them may provide the basic information you will need in order to put together some preliminary plans. These initial plans will enable you to think about and design strategies to help make the experience productive for both you and the group. For example, I was recently asked to help a group that was charged with designing its school district's staff development plan. Before coming to the session, I talked with the chairperson of this group and found out that one of the members had a reputation for taking the rest of the group off task during the discussions. The leader of this group had told me that this behavior was very annoying to the other group members. In preparing my plan for this group, I added a list of ground rules I shared with the members. One of these ground rules was that off-topic discussions should be kept to a minimum. I also picked up from the leader's comments that this group could be shutting out some of the valuable ideas that the member who had the off-task reputation brought to the table because of his past behavior. Taking all these factors into account helped me to develop a plan to facilitate this group and balance the negative situations. I decided to address the topic of staying on task at the beginning of the meeting and be ready with a reflective paraphrase and a redirective statement if he tried to take the group off task. I used both strategies to keep the meeting focused.

Event Strategies

Many facilitators find that even with a well-prepared plan, they still run into issues. These facilitators utilize techniques that help them to gather information about the group as members are entering, connecting, and beginning to work together. Here are some ways to gather information about the members of the group you will be working with as the session begins.

♦ Stand by the door to the meeting room and personally welcome group members. This not only sets a good tone but lets you assess the emotions and personalities of the members you will be facilitating.

- ◆ Listen for member comments as you are preparing to start the meeting.
- ◆ Watch the informal interaction among group members as they get ready for the meeting. Which members talk to others in the room? Who seems connected to others? Which members avoid conversations with others? Who seems to have the most power in the group?
- ◆ Keep an eye out for informal seating patterns. Do some people sit in the front of the room or in the back? How much personal space do the members require of each other? Does there seem to be "assigned seats" for group members?
- ◆ Observe people's reactions during the opening activities of the meeting. Do people freely participate, or is their involvement labored? When asked to share, do they contain their comments to a small number of members they seem comfortable with, or do they branch out to everyone in the group?
- ◆ Watch the body language of group members

Welcoming Group Members

Effective facilitators find it beneficial to stand by the door and welcome team members as they enter the room. During this time, the facilitator is able to begin to build the rapport necessary to effectively work with this team during the session. Another benefit of this welcoming activity is that the facilitator is able to observe the behavior of people as they enter the room. Many people wear their emotions on their sleeves, and while you are standing by the door, you may notice that people have not yet had a chance to put on their game face that they will use in the meeting. It is an opportune time to see these people in their real emotional state before they enter the room and join the group. As you welcome people to the session, make mental notes about the kind of emotions you are picking up from your initial conversations. For example, let's say that as you are standing outside the room welcoming people, you notice that several of the members seem to be angry or disconnected. In order to get people talking to each other, you decide to change your opening to have each person share a positive event from the week. As the people on the team share this opening, you begin to notice the anger dissipating from the room. They are now ready to work together.

Listening for Group Comments

For most sessions, team members usually arrive 10 to 15 minutes early. During this time, they tend to mingle and warm up to each other.

This time provides you with an opportunity to walk around and listen in on these conversations, and you'll be able to pick up small clues and indicators of the group's emotions and interest in regard to your facilitation session. The key here is to be subtle, not obvious. For example, as you walk around, scan the group with your eyes and your ears. Don't stop, lean in, or stare at any individual or group for extended periods of time. Your goal here is to get a general idea of the group's emotions rather than specific, detailed information.

Once you've taken the pulse of the group, step off to the side and think through your plan for this session. Do the strategies and activities you have put together match the needs that you are picking up as you walk around? If not, make some adjustments in your planning. For example, let's say that as you are walking around, you hear a lot of discussion about a situation involving a parent at one of the schools. As the facilitator, you might choose to open the session by saying, "I understand that there has been a lot of anxiety in the school district in regard to the parent situation here at Hoover Elementary School. Before we start our meeting today, let's take 10 minutes to talk about the situation and how it's been resolved."

The facilitator in this situation has listened to many comments during the mingling portion of the meeting. He decided that the negative emotions associated with this situation would get in the way of the effectiveness of this team. Because of this, he decided that it was best to take a few minutes to clear the air before starting the meeting.

In another situation, a different facilitator may decide, after hearing this kind of discussion as it informally occurs, to use a different approach. This facilitator may say, "I understand that there has been a lot of anxiety over the situation at Hoover Elementary School. Since there's not much information out about this yet, we need to put it aside in order to finish the work that we are charged with completing today. If we get additional information or if we have time at the end of the day, we could take a few minutes to discuss this situation."

In this section, you have seen how two facilitators have handled a similar situation in different ways. As you will find in most facilitation situations, there is no one right way to deal with a potential problem. The strategies you choose to use will depend on your diagnosis and perception of the situation. In the final analysis, you need to be observing how the group handles your strategy to determine if it was helpful to the group's operation.

Watch for Seating Patterns

Once the initial mingling is over, group members need to find a place to sit within their team. While some teams have assigned seating locations, others allow their members to sit wherever they want. As people begin to find seating locations, watch for patterns to emerge. For example, in some situations, team members want to sit far away from the front of the room. They may choose these spots for many reasons. Some team members don't like to be at the center of attention; others may have work they would like to complete and they sit away from the front thinking that no one will notice that they are not engaged in the process. Some group members will sit together to provide each other with emotional and power support. These group members may sit together in voting factions or coalitions. At times, you will also notice that certain members are isolated from any group. These members may come in later than the rest and sit alone.

In one situation, a group of team members sat in a semicircle. The group facilitator worked from the open part of the circle and the group members faced each other as they held their discussion. One of the group members who had a reputation for being confrontational and uncooperative chose to sit outside the semicircle behind the rest of the group members. As ideas were discussed, this isolated team member would throw negative comments into the discussion. This behavior took the rest of the team off task. In a follow-up session, the group facilitator watched as the same seating pattern began to emerge. This time, however, the facilitator had prepared for the negative actions of this team member. She laid out strict ground rules in regard to when oppositional comments could be shared with the team. In future sessions, this facilitator also set up the seating arrangement so it that would be impossible for this team member to sit outside the circle and throw stones at the comments and ideas made by other team members.

Observe Initial Activity Behavior

Usually in a facilitation session the group is engaged in some type of opening activity to start the session. As group members are connecting and completing these opening activities, watch for both verbal and non-verbal clues in regard to the emotions of the group. Let's say that a facilitator has asked the group to stand up, find a partner, and talk about the past progress of this team. As this activity is unfolding, the facilitator notices that two of the pairs have refused to talk. This behavior could cause problems during the rest of the meeting. The facilitator needs to be thinking of ways to get these people involved in later discussions. She might have group members write their responses on paper, put their ideas on sticky pads, or ask each individual to share one idea with the entire team. By observing how people participate in the initial activities of a facilitation session, the facilitator receives important information that can be used to help this team become even more effective during its session.

In another example, the facilitator notices that today the group is very active and engaged in sharing ideas during an opening activity. Now the facilitator thinks about how to expand his participation activities to take advantage of this situation. Instead of just having team members write down their ideas and share one with the group, he decides to have them involved in an open brainstorming session. This brainstorming takes advantage of the emotional state that this group is in today.

As a facilitator, it's crucial to engage the group in some type of active learning activity during the early stages of its team meeting. Not only does this provide you with an important diagnostic opportunity, but it also sets the stage or norms for active group engagement during the facilitation process. Later, I explore strategies that can be used in opening a session with the group.

Observe Body Language

People are driven by their emotions. They may say one thing but inside are feeling something else. People may be able to mask the verbal portion of their feelings, but they are usually less successful in covering up the nonverbal indicators of their emotions. Begin a facilitation session by continually scanning the group members to see how they are feeling through their body language. While positive nonverbal messages may be present, the negative nonverbal indicators may be most apparent to you as you facilitate this group. For example, when you take time to highlight the agenda for the day, you may notice some group members sitting back and rolling their eyes. This could be an indication that they are upset or frustrated with the agenda or portions of the agenda. It could also indicate that they are upset with the actions of other team members. Whatever the root cause of their problems, it's important for you to make note of these nonverbal indicators. As you facilitate the session, keep an eye on these people to make sure that they do not get out of control or cause problems with other team members. You might want to move your facilitation area closer to these people, or you might want to stand away from them so that attention is not drawn to their behaviors.

In a related situation, you may notice that when the group is generating possibilities for a solution, a couple of team members have a scowl on their faces. As mentioned before, you do not know for certain the origin of this problem, but it is something for you to keep an eye on as you are working with this group. Some facilitators use nonverbal indicators to get a clear sense of the emotional state of the group they are working with at the present time. They use this data to make decisions in regard to activities, groupings, and the pacing of the decision-making process.

While it is important to use nonverbal or body language indicators to give you some sense of the emotional state of the group you are facilitating, be careful not to let this information steer you away from productive problem resolution. When you notice that several members of the team seem to be angry or disconnected with the process, you may need to move this group forward in the productive resolution of a decision. Use the information you are gathering from body language and nonverbal emotional indicators to help you maximize the success of your group.

STARTING A SESSION

A big key to your success in facilitating a difficult group is how you start the session. The initial tone you set goes a long way in helping a difficult group connect. Many facilitators use a variety of techniques to help people emotionally connect during the facilitation session. In this section, I examine several of these ideas to help you as you begin to facilitate a difficult group of people.

Physical Room Setup

Detailed information about the physical setup of a meeting room is explained in Chapter 2. In this section, I examine physical space issues in regard to working with difficult groups. For a more general description of space considerations and their impact on groups in general, see Chapter 2.

In thinking about the space needs of a difficult group, it is important to understand the nature of the group's difficulty. One group may need to be placed in a small, close circle to keep the members connected and the tone of their discussion conversational; another group may require being divided into small cluster teams to deal with relationship issues; a third group may need to be placed in rows so that the group members can listen to the facilitator and keep their interaction at a minimum. Choose the arrangement you feel will keep the group from getting out of control while allowing it to work together and learn how to get along.

Another factor to consider in regard to physical space is the emotional feel of the room. Rooms can have emotional baggage that will rub off on participants in a facilitation session. This emotional baggage can be either positive or negative, depending on the perception of the participants. Here are some examples to illustrate the point:

1. As a new assistant superintendent in a school district, I was asked to lead a meeting of a school curriculum decision-making council. The meeting was held in a room that was unused except

for board meetings. It was a block wall room with windows that looked out over a small field. There was nothing on the walls, and the table in the front of the room was set up for upcoming board meetings. In running the meeting, I noticed that the participants had a lot of trouble coming to consensus on any ideas. Several of them appeared to be uncomfortable and anxious during the meeting. I stopped the meeting and asked the members what was wrong. Nobody would respond. We continued to meet but got nothing major accomplished. After the meeting, I scheduled private meetings with some of the members of the curriculum council. They told me that several of the teachers had experienced negative situations in that room as a result of the actions of the board of education. This was getting in the way of their comfort in working together in the room. In the future, meetings of this group were held in a smaller, more intimate classroom location with much better results.

2. As a school principal, I always took the emotional energy of the room into consideration in planning meetings. We had to work through a series of budget cuts over the years. In bringing a team together to consider these cuts, we used the same space during each of the sessions. Once the primary ideas were generated, we would hold a staff meeting in another room that we used for announcements. This helped to contain the emotional responses of the staff, since they had normally received news in this room. When we were meeting to generate new ideas or to celebrate our successes, we chose a third meeting space. After a time, our staff's emotions were shaped by these meeting rooms. It helped to contain the negativity normally associated with the various tasks we had to deal with as a team.

Keep in mind the emotional baggage or feeling that a room has to offer when you are anticipating working with a difficult team or group. It can be one factor that has an impact on your success as a facilitator.

As you begin to work with a difficult group of people, keep in mind the important role that the meeting location plays in the success of this group. One other reason the group you are working with may be difficult could be because of the meeting location. Take some time to talk to team members to find out any unknown history or emotions associated with the meeting location.

Here are some general points to keep in mind in regard to room emotions and facilitating a difficult group:

- ◆ Match the physical space for the meeting to the emotional needs of the group; use the space to help the group grow as a collaborative team.
- ◆ Keep in mind that some rooms have a certain amount of emotional resonance or dissonance associated with them. Pick a room that will maximize your group's emotional success.
- ◆ Watch the group members as they work together. Change the physical arrangement or space as needed to keep them on track emotionally.
- ◆ When working with a group that has the potential to be negative, it's a good idea to have members sit in close proximity to each other. By being close to each other, they are less likely to get mad. If they are far apart, there is less intimacy, plus they may have to raise their voice to be heard. This could lead to group members shouting in the meetings.

MUSIC AND DIFFICULT GROUPS

It was once said that music can calm the savage beast. The same can be said for music and difficult groups. Music and its impact on facilitating groups in general is a topic that is discussed in Chapter 3. In this section, I examine ideas about music that directly relate to managing difficult teams or groups.

In general, many people resonate well to appropriate music. It not only connects to people, but it also helps to break their normal thought patterns, one of the contributing factors of a difficult team of people. For example, the following was reported by a teacher assigned to meet with a group of staff members who had a reputation for being difficult when discussing specific procedures for an upcoming high school graduation.

> In setting up the meeting room, I had thought about having some light music playing in the background as the teachers I was meeting with entered. I noticed that some people had arrived at the meeting with a scowl on their face, but were less visibly upset once they heard the music. I chose an instrumental CD of top hits of the 1960s and 1970s that encompassed the relative age group of these teachers. The meeting started off a lot more positively than I had experienced when I worked with this group in the past.

Music should be used in a strategic manner to help set the right kind of tone when working with a difficult group. Keep these questions in mind when using music with a potentially difficult group:

◆ What kinds of negative behaviors do you anticipate in your group? Will the group need to be motivated or calmed down to help it be less difficult? What specific parts of the meeting might benefit from music?

◆ List the generations that are represented by your group members.

◆ What kinds of music do you anticipate might be soothing or motivating for your group?

◆ Within each type of music, what specific songs do you plan to use in starting your session? What other songs will you use and at what other times do you plan to use this music?

◆ How will you manage the technology needed to use music in your session?

FOUNDATION-SETTING ACTIVITIES

Facilitators often use a strategy called a foundation-setting activity to establish the proper tone for a meeting. The concept of foundation setting was first presented in Chapter 3. They can be particularly helpful in dealing with negative groups. Here are some ways that foundation-setting activities can help a difficult group:

◆ They help set a positive tone for the meeting.

◆ They allow all group members to speak and have their voices heard.

◆ They allow group members to set their expectations for the meeting.

◆ When facilitators use foundation-setting activities, they model positive group processes that their team can use in future meetings.

1. A medium-sized district formed a task force that will look at the curriculum cycles and make recommendations for their implementation. This team has decided it will hold its meetings after school. During the day, the professional staff on this committee has experienced two disruptive students, an angry parent, a shortage of teaching materials in one classroom, and an unplanned fire drill. Two of the members had their yearly performance review with their principal. All these situations have caused some level of stress and anxiety for the team members on this task force. In order for them to be productive in working with the curriculum cycle implementation project, they need to find a way to empty these negative emotions from their thought process.

2. Another team is working to put together a staff recognition program. This team is comprised of professional staff, parents, community members, and representatives from local industry. They choose to meet evenings after dinner. Before coming to this team meeting, most of these members had to prepare dinner, work with their children in completing their homework, or deal with other family-related stresses. These negative emotions hold the potential to impact the effectiveness of this team as it works to complete its assigned task.

In both of these situations, the facilitator in charge chose to use a foundation-setting activity to reshape the emotional thought process of the session participants. A foundation-setting activity is designed to completely reshape the thinking of facilitation participants. Foundation-setting activities usually have the following common components:

- They occur at the beginning of a meeting.
- They get everyone's voice into the room.
- They utilize the prior knowledge each participant brings to the meeting.
- They establish a positive tone/energy level.

Here's an example of a foundation-setting activity that was successfully used with a difficult group recently:

In this foundation-setting activity, the facilitator had written the following directions on a chart tablet that was posted in the front of a room where a facilitation session was about to occur:
At 9:30 A.M., be ready to share the following:

- Your name/role
- Something positive that happened in your classroom today
- One idea you hope to gain as a result of today's meeting

Since this foundation-setting activity was used with a large group, each member was asked to share the ideas in groups of three while the facilitator walked around to the small groups listening for insights. With smaller teams, the sharing can occur individually within the entire group. This opening fits the criteria for an effective foundation-setting activity, since it gets everyone's voice in the room, utilizes prior knowledge of the participants, and establishes a positive tone for the meeting. The middle prompt, asking the participants to share something positive from their classroom, is designed to reshape their thinking into a positive mode.

When people are asked to generate a positive example, it becomes harder for them to get negative in a meeting.

Here is another example:

At the beginning of the meeting, the facilitator verbally shared the following: "Today, we will start our meeting with a brief opening. This opening is designed to give us more information about each other that we need to know as we work together. Take 30 seconds and jot down your responses to the following:

♦ Share something about yourself that very few others in the room would know.
♦ Talk about a success you have had in the last 2 weeks either in your personal or professional life.
♦ Discuss what you would like to accomplish as a result of this meeting and how you will work to make that desire happen."

This foundation-setting activity is slightly different from the first example. The facilitator knew that group members had worked together for a period of time and is helping participants to move to a deeper personal knowledge level when he asks them to share something about themselves that few other people in the room would know.

The second part of the foundation-setting activity is where the frame of reference of the participants is shifted to the positive. In this example, the facilitator has broadened the prompt to include either something positive from the group members' personal or professional life. This broadening allows the participants to select the example that is most motivating to them. It also eliminates the situation where someone could say, "Nothing positive has happened in my classroom during the last 2 weeks." When a group is given a broad prompt such as this, the facilitator finds that about half of the responses are personal and half are professional. These responses provide valuable information for the participants, but also the facilitator gains insights into team members' thinking.

The third section of this foundation-setting activity is designed to go beyond just finding out what participants desire from the meeting. This prompt is also designed to begin to build participant commitment to making their desires happen. In the first example, the facilitator just asked participants to share their hope for the meeting. This helped the facilitator gauge how far he could push the group. The second example not only provides that kind of information, but it also asked for participants to publicly state their role in making these desires happen. When people publicly state that they will do something, there is a higher chance that they will work to make it happen, since they have gone out on a limb with their statement.

As participants share how they will help these desires come true, facilitators need to make note either mentally or physically so that they can use this information later to hold the group accountable for its success.

In a third example, a facilitator uses a foundation-setting activity in a different manner to start a group. In this situation, a task force was formed to study a new curricular program. The program was controversial, and many of the team members had negative feelings about it and about being on the team. The facilitator decided it was best to get these feelings out on the table. Here is how he started the meeting:

> As people are coming into a room to attend a meeting regarding a new, controversial curriculum program, the facilitator has the following written on a chart:
>   At 7:30 P.M., be ready to
>
> ♦ Introduce yourself and share your role in the district and on this team.
> ♦ Share a positive experience you've had with one aspect of our school curriculum over the last couple of years.
> ♦ Tell us your greatest fear associated with this new curricular program.
>
> (We'll be talking through these as we move through the meeting)

In this example, the facilitator stood at a chart and wrote down people's fears as they shared them, without making any comments. Once all the fears were listed, the facilitator used this chart as a teaching tool for the group. He asked group members to look over the chart and identify the general trends they noticed in the concerns. Then she had the group members meet in groups of three to discuss these trends and their danger to the new curricular program. Finally, she had these groups of three generate strategies to overcome these fears. This was a very productive exercise for this task force because it was able to openly present problems but was also able to generate possible solutions for these areas. In the opening section of the meeting, the group was able to solve about a third of the concerns that were expressed. The facilitator posted the chart of concerns in front of the room so the members could scan it during the meeting. By the end of the meeting, about two thirds of the concerns had been addressed by the group.

When facilitating a difficult or angry group, it is important to help members empty themselves of negative emotions or feelings. Once these emotions are released by the team members, they need to be placed somewhere. By using the chart, the facilitator in this example gave the group members participating in the discussion a location in which to place their feelings of concern. The use of the chart also kept task force members from transferring these negative emotions to the facilitator.

In working with a team that was evaluating the school improvement plan for a school site, a facilitator noticed that two factions were forming within this team. She could tell that people were getting angry at each other, because she picked up changes in voice tone and body language. She decided it was time to stop the discussion and set a new foundation for the group. As the group finished its discussion, she stepped off to the side and wrote the following directions on chart paper:

Take a minute to respond to the following ideas:

1. Specifically, what progress has our group made today in relation to the school improvement process?

2. What communication difficulties seem to be inhibiting us from making further progress?

3. How do we overcome these difficulties in order to move forward?

This facilitator told the group members that they appeared to be stuck on the issue and needed to take a moment to refine their thoughts. She turned the chart toward the group members and asked them to stand and talk with a partner about the three questions she had posted on the chart. Next she allowed each pair to share their ideas with the entire group. She wrote down their responses to Question 3 and helped the members come to a consensus on the strategies they would use to keep their communication channels open. Whenever the members began to experience difficulties in communication, this facilitator referred them back to the chart and reminded them of their agreement to continue open discussion.

FRAMING

A second skill that facilitators use to set the proper tone in working with difficult groups is called framing. Framing was introduced in Chapter 3 and can be specific or general in nature but usually contains the following components:

♦ A recognition statement naming the prevailing concern of the group
♦ A focusing statement reminding the group of its designated task or assignment

♦ A statement letting the group know when the prevailing concern will be addressed

This framing statement was used by a facilitator working with a group that was supposed to be working on a districtwide staff development program but was preoccupied with the possible district budget cuts. As you read the framing statement, look for the three components listed above.

> "I understand that many people are concerned about the possibility of budget cuts. For now, however, our job is to continue the development of the district staff development plan. At the end of the day, we'll take a few minutes to discuss your questions and fears surrounding the budget situation. As the day progresses, please write down your thoughts and questions concerning the budget situation on the chart in the back of the room. When we talk about the budget problems later in the day, we'll try to address as many of your questions and concerns as we can at this time."

This framing statement kept the group members on task for the entire day. Writing their budget concerns on a chart lowered their anxiety and allowed the district leaders to see the issues the group had about the budget. During a lunch break, the administrative team was able to use these concerns and questions to generate a meaningful presentation that helped to alleviate many of the fears expressed by this group. The group members were satisfied with the explanation of the budget situation, and many were glad that they had waited to get the most accurate information. Here is a summary of the steps the facilitator took to couple the use of a foundation-setting activity and framing to help a team get back on task.

1. At the beginning of the meeting, the facilitator listened to the group, capturing the concerns of the members. She picked these up during the foundation-setting activity part of the meeting.

2. After picking up their concerns, she designed a framing statement to get the concerns out on the table. Her statement was, "Since there are a lot of concerns in the team right now, let's take the next 10 minutes and list them on a piece of chart paper."

3. Once these concerns were listed out, she put together a process for the group to address its needs in relation to the concern. She told the group she would leave the concerns posted and at each break period she would go over to the list and cross out those concerns that had been addressed by the team in its meeting.

4. Finally, she was able to move the members beyond their initial concerns and back to their assigned topic, since she provided them with a place to "put" their concerns. This helped the team move on and hold a productive meeting.

This framing statement used by this facilitator was very simple but worked well for her in this example. In designing and using a framing statement, it is important that you have some knowledge of the group and use this knowledge in generating the frame. Watch how this plays out in the following example:

"This morning, as we were preparing to start the meeting, I over-heard several people commenting about their concerns in con-junction with the construction project going on in our building. While this project has nothing to do with our task this morning, which is to solve the articulation problem between grade levels, we'll take the first 10 minutes of the day to discuss this issue. Once this time is up, we will need to take the issue off our plates and focus the rest of the day on solving the articulation problem."

The facilitator was very specific about the fact that the concern had nothing to do with the topic that the team was called together to discuss. The facilitator was also specific about the fact that the discussion about this concern was only going to take 10 minutes away from the group's assignment. The group was allowed to talk about the topic for 10 minutes, but the facilitator laid out a structure for this discussion. She chose one of the group members to act as a note taker. She gave the group 5 minutes to share its concerns and then 5 minutes to generate some possible solutions in regard to the situation. The note taker was able to write down a short statement summarizing each concern. The facilitator monitored the dis-cussion and kept the group on track. Since she was not in charge of writ-ing down the concerns, she was able to concentrate on the emotions of the group and the process of sharing concerns. In the end, the group came up with two ideas to help ease its concerns during the construction process.

Framing statements also help set up the group if it should stray off task during the discussion. If the facilitator has opened a meeting with the proper framing statement, this facilitator now has permission to bring the group back to task. See how this works in the following examples.

In a situation where a group is working to understand the most recent set of state achievement test scores, members of the group begin to bring up off-task objections that justify the scores. The facilitator decides that this discussion will take the group off its assigned task and shares the following framing statement:

> "I understand your concerns around the issues you have brought up in our discussion. At this time, however, we can't control these issues, and our task is to put together our diagnosis of the most recent test information available to our district. We are limited in relation to the time we have to complete this task. Let me jot down these two concerns and let's take a few minutes right before lunch to talk about strategies we would like to employ to address these concerns."

In this situation, the mid-meeting framing worked to get the group back on task. In some situations, a mid-meeting statement such as this only works for a few minutes. An overly anxious team may come back to its concern several times. In working with this type of team, it may be necessary for the facilitator to periodically use shortened framing statements to get the group back on task. In relation to our first example, let's say that the concerns kept coming up in the discussion. The facilitator might make statements such as these:

1. "Remember, we will address those concerns when we are ready for lunch."

2. "I can see this is an area of great concern, but we need to keep moving forward toward our goal."

3. "Obviously, these topics are getting in the way of our ability to move forward on our task. Let's stop here and deal with these concerns before moving forward. In doing this, however, we need to understand that we will not get very far on our goals for the day."

Framing statements have the potential to keep a team on track and focused on its agenda. They can also help a team deal with anger and anxiety. Keep them in mind as you work with difficult groups.

USE OF AN AGENDA

In working with a difficult group, the use of an agenda is a powerful tool that can help you keep the group on task and productive. Sometimes individuals in a difficult group are interested in causing problems to keep others from being productive. Agendas serve an important role in dealing with difficult teams. The following are examples of how they help in working with difficult teams:

1. Agendas help to format the thinking of group members. Some groups need a tightly controlled agenda, while others benefit from a looser agenda.

2. If you have a group that is comprised of clock watchers, consider having an agenda without specific times to free the group to spend more time on needed topics.

3. If your group tends to wander and not get much done, consider putting specific times on the agenda to hold them accountable to stay on track.

4. In developing the agenda, let the group have input into the process. This can be done at the session to allow all members a voice in the direction of the meeting.

SUMMARY

Difficulties with individuals and whole groups can cause problems for facilitators in the conduct of meetings. In cases where problems arise, it is important that the facilitator take an active role in engaging the conflict and getting the group on track. This chapter presents a series of ideas that can work with either a whole team or an individual on a team. Some of the strategies are subtle, while others are very direct in their application. The facilitator should keep in mind that it is important to use the least intrusive strategy to address the issue at hand. If a simple redirective gesture gets the group back on track, the intervention should stop there.

Something else that the facilitator should keep in mind is the fact that the strategies presented here are situational in nature. Each idea should be analyzed and tested to see how it impacts a particular group or situation before it is totally integrated by the facilitator. This can be accomplished by trying out a small part of a potential strategy with a group or getting the perceptions of a representative group in an agenda-planning session.

Whatever the method used to deal with a difficult group, facilitators will find that getting a handle on the behaviors of difficult team members will make their life and the lives of those on the team more productive and pleasant.

References

Doyle, M., & Straus, D. (1982/1993). *How to make meetings work.* New York: Berkley.

Elgin, Suzette. (1993). *The gentle art of verbal self-defense.* New York: Barnes & Noble.

Garmston, R., & Wellman, B. (1992). *How to make presentations that teach and transform.* Alexandria, VA: Association for Supervision and Curriculum Development.

Garmston, R., & Wellman, B. (1997). *The adaptive school: Developing and facilitating collaborative groups.* El Dorado Hills, CA: Four Hats.

Garmston, R., & Wellman, B. (1999). *The adaptive school: A sourcebook for developing collaborative groups.* Norwood, MA: Christopher-Gordon.

Goleman, D., Boyatzis, R., & McKee, A. (2002). *Primal leadership: realizing the power of emotional intelligence.* Boston: Harvard Business School Press.

Hargrove, R. (1995). *Masterful coaching: Extraordinary results by impacting people and the way they think and work together.* San Francisco: Jossey-Bass.

Jackson, T. (1999). *More activities that teach.* Cedar City, UT: Red Rock.

Justice, T., & Jamieson, D. (1999). *The facilitator's fieldbook.* New York: American Management Association.

Kaner, S. (1996). *The facilitator's guide to participatory decision-making.* Gabriola Island, BC, Canada: New Society.

Lipton, L., & Wellman, B. (1998). *Pathways to understanding: Patterns and practices in the learner-focused classroom.* Guilford, VT: Pathways.

Marzano, R., Pickering, D., & Pollock, J. (2001). *Classroom instruction that works.* Alexandria, VA: Association for Supervision and Curriculum Development.

Midura, D., & Glover, D. (1995). *More team building challenges.* Champaign, IL: Human Kinetics.

Newstrom, J., & Scannel, E. (1998). *The big book of team building games: Trust-building activities, team spirit exercises, and other fun things to do.* New York: McGraw-Hill.

Peck, M. Scott. (1987). *The different drum: Community making and peace.* New York: Touchstone.

Robbins, H., & Finley, M. (1995). *Why teams don't work: What went wrong and how to make it right.* Princeton, NJ: Peterson's/Pacesetter.

Schmoker, M. (2001). *The results fieldbook: Practical strategies from dramatically improved schools.* Alexandria, VA: Association for Supervision and Curriculum Development.

Senge, P., Ross, R., Kleiner, A., Roberts, C., & Smith, B. (1994). *The fifth discipline fieldbook: Strategies and tools for building a learning organization.* New York: Doubleday.

Toastmasters International. (1982). *Gestures: Your body speaks.* Mission Viejo, CA: Author.

Wheatley, M. (1994). *Leadership and the new science: Learning about organization from an orderly universe.* San Francisco: Berrett-Koehler.

Wohlstetter, P., Van Kirk, A., Robertson, P., & Mohrman, S. (1997). *Organizing for successful school-based management.* Alexandria, VA: Association for Supervision and Curriculum Development.

Index

Page references followed by *t* indicates a table; followed by *fig* indicates an illustrated figure.

CORWIN PRESS

The Corwin Press logo—a raven striding across an open book—represents the union of courage and learning. Corwin Press is committed to improving education for all learners by publishing books and other professional development resources for those serving the field of K–12 education. By providing practical, hands-on materials, Corwin Press continues to carry out the promise of its motto: **"Helping Educators Do Their Work Better."**